# THE
# NO-
# SUGAR
# Cookbook

# THE NO-SUGAR Cookbook

Delicious recipes to make
your mouth water . . .
all sugar-free!

Series Editor: Kimberly A. Tessmer, R.D., L.D.

Adams Media
Avon, Massachusetts

Published by
Adams Media,
an F+W Publications Company
57 Littlefield Street
Avon, MA 02322
www.adamsmedia.com

ISBN 10: 1-59869-203-8
ISBN 13: 978-1-59869-203-7

Printed in the United States of America.

J  I  H  G  F  E  D  C  B  A

**Library of Congress Cataloging-in-Publication Data**
Tessmer, Kimberly A.
The no-sugar cookbook / Kimberly A. Tessmer.
p.        cm.
Includes index.
ISBN-13: 978-1-59869-203-7
ISBN-10: 1-59869-203-8
1. Sugar-free diet—Recipes. I. Title.
RM237.85.T47 2006
641.5'638—dc22
2006028443

This publication is designed to provide accurate and authoritative information with regard to the subject matter covered. It is sold with the understanding that the publisher is not engaged in rendering legal, accounting, or other professional advice. If legal advice or other expert assistance is required, the services of a competent professional person should be sought.

—From a *Declaration of Principles* jointly adopted by a Committee of the American Bar Association and a Committee of Publishers and Associations

Many of the designations used by manufacturers and sellers to distinguish their product are claimed as trademarks. Where those designations appear in this book and Adams Media was aware of a trademark claim, the designations have been printed with initial capital letters.

Contains portions of material adapted or abridged from *The Everything® Diabetes Cookbook* by Pamela Rice Hahn, ©2002, F+W Publications, Inc.

*The No-Sugar Cookbook* is intended as a reference volume only, not as a medical manual. In light of the complex, individual, and specific nature of heath problems, this book is not intended to replace professional medical advice. The ideas, procedures, and suggestions in this book are intended to supplement, not replace, the advice of a trained medical professional. Consult your physician before adopting the suggestions in this book. The author and publisher disclaim any liability arising directly or indirectly from the use of this book.

*This book is available at quantity discounts for bulk purchases.*
*For information, please call 1-800-289-0963.*

# Introduction

Many of us are born with a natural sweet tooth. After all, sugar can offer a tasty addition to meals and snacks. On the other hand, if you are not careful, it can also add plenty of additional calories, which if you eat more than you need, can cause unhealthy weight gain. There are no vitamins, minerals, or other essential nutrients in sugar itself and therefore, it is frequently referred to as "empty calories."

There is a difference between "added sugars" and "natural sugars." Added sugars are just that—sugars that are added to foods and beverages during processing and/or preparation such as soft drinks, baked goods, and candy bars. Natural sugars are sugars that are naturally found in foods such as fruit (in the form of fructose) and dairy products (in the form of lactose). The body cannot distinguish between natural sugar and added sugar. However, foods containing natural sugar are additionally packed with vitamins, minerals, and other nutrients essential for good health, while most foods containing added sugars tend to be high in calories and low in key nutrients. On a positive note, a little added sugar can enhance the taste of some foods, whole-grain cereal, for example that some people may otherwise resist. The key is moderation and minimizing "empty calorie" foods.

As a substitute to sugar, many people make a personal choice to use products such as Splenda, which can be found in many processed foods and can be used as a substitute for sugar in countless recipes. These types of sugar substitutes are considered GRAS or Generally Recognized As Safe by the FDA (U.S. Food and Drug Administration) as well as other national regulatory agencies. The American Dietetic Association states that, "consumers can safely enjoy a range of nutritive and non-nutritive sweeteners when consumed in a diet that is guided by current federal nutrition recommendations, such as the Dietary Guidelines for Americans and the Dietary Reference Intakes, as well as individual health goals."

There are all types of reasons people may want or need to follow a no-added-sugar diet including weight loss, diabetes, other health problems, and personal choices. Whatever your reasons for wanting to decrease the amount of sugar in your diet, our goal with *The No-Sugar Cookbook* is to help you indulge your sweet cravings with recipes that are healthful, tasty and will minimize the addition of added sugars in your diet.

# Salsas, Sauces, and Shortcuts

## chapter one

# Toasted Sesame Seeds

**Yields ½ cup**
**Serving size: 1 tsp.**

½ cup white sesame seeds
¼ teaspoon sea salt (optional)

---

**NUTRITIONAL ANALYSIS**
(per serving):

Calories: 15
Protein: trace
Carbohydrate: 1 g
Fat: 1 g
Sat. Fat: trace
Cholesterol: 0 mg
Sodium: 26 mg
Fiber: trace
Exchange Approx.:
½ Fat

1. Add the sesame seeds to a nonstick skillet over low heat. Toast until golden, shaking the pan or stirring the mixture frequently so that the seeds toast evenly. (The seeds will swell slightly during the toasting process.) When the aroma of the sesame seeds becomes evident and they've reached a light brown color, remove from the heat and pour into a bowl. Add the sea salt and mix well. Set aside and allow to cool.

2. Once cooled, grind using a mortar and pestle or blender, and season to taste. Store in an airtight container.

## Toasting Frenzy

Many nuts, including pine nuts, almonds, and even sunflower seeds, toast well. Simply follow the recipe for Toasted Sesame Seeds. Store them, whole or ground, in an airtight container.

# Asian Gingered Almonds

1. Preheat oven to 350°F. In a microwave-safe bowl, mix the butter, Bragg's Liquid Aminos, and ginger. Microwave on high for 30 seconds, or until the butter is melted; blend well.

2. Spread the almonds on a shallow baking sheet treated with nonstick spray. Bake for 12 to 15 minutes or until light gold, stirring occasionally.

3. Pour the seasoned butter over the almonds, and stir to mix. Bake an additional 5 minutes. Store in airtight containers in cool place.

## Good Fat!

Almonds and many other nuts fall within the "good fats" category because they are low in unhealthy, saturated fats.

**Yields 1 cup**
**Serving size: 1 tbs.**

2 teaspoons unsalted butter
1 tablespoon Bragg's Liquid Aminos
1 teaspoon ground ginger
1 cup slivered almonds

**NUTRITIONAL ANALYSIS**
(per serving):

Calories: 58
Protein: 2 g
Carbohydrate: 2 g
Fat: 5 g
Sat. Fat: 1 g
Cholesterol: 1 mg
Sodium: 44 mg
Fiber: 1 g
Exchange Approx.:
1½ Fats

# Almond Spread

**Yields ½ cup**
**Serving size: 1 tbs.**

¼ cup ground, raw almonds
2 teaspoons honey
4 teaspoons water
Pinch of salt (optional)

**NUTRITIONAL ANALYSIS**
(per serving, without salt):

Calories: 30
Protein: 1 g
Carbohydrate: 3 g
Fat: 2 g
Sat. Fat: trace
Cholesterol: 0 mg
Sodium: trace
Fiber: trace
Exchange Approx.:
½ Fat

In a blender, combine all ingredients and process until smooth.

## Toasted Almond Seasoning

Add an extra flavor dimension to salads, rice dishes, or vegetables by sprinkling some toasted almonds over the top of the dish. Toast ½ cup ground raw almonds in a nonstick skillet over low heat, stirring frequently until they are a light brown color. Store the cooled almonds in an airtight container in a cool, dry place. This low-sodium substitute has only 16 calories per teaspoon, and counts as a ½ Fat Exchange Approximation.

# Horseradish Mustard

Combine the ingredients in a food processor or blender and process until smooth. Pour into a decorative jar and store in the refrigerator.

## The Vinegar-Oil Balancing Act

The easiest way to tame too much vinegar is to add some vegetable oil. Because oil adds fat, the better alternative is to start with less vinegar and add it gradually to the recipe until you arrive at a flavor you prefer.

**Yields ¾ cup**
**Serving size: 1 tsp.**

¼ cup dry mustard
2½ tablespoons prepared horseradish
1 teaspoon sea salt
¼ cup white wine vinegar
1 tablespoon olive oil
Cayenne pepper to taste (optional)

---

**NUTRITIONAL ANALYSIS**
(per serving):

Calories: 10
Protein: trace
Carbohydrate: 1 g
Fat: 1 g
Sat. Fat: trace
Cholesterol: 0 mg
Sodium: 70 mg
Fiber: trace
Exchange Approx.:
1 Free Condiment

# Piccalilli

**Yields 2 quarts**
**Serving size: 2 tbs.**

1 cup chopped green
   tomatoes
1½ cups chopped cabbage
1 cup white onions
1 cup chopped cauliflower
1 cup chopped cucumber
½ cup chopped red pepper
½ cup chopped green pepper
1½ cups apple cider or white
   vinegar
¾ cup Splenda granular
½ teaspoon turmeric
1 teaspoon ginger
1½ teaspoons dried mustard
1½ teaspoons mustard seed
1 teaspoon celery seed
1 sachet pickling spices
¼ cup pickling salt
Pickled onions to taste
   (optional)

---

**NUTRITIONAL ANALYSIS**
(per serving, without salt):

Calories: 17
Protein: trace
Carbohydrate: 4 g
Fat: trace
Sat. Fat: trace
Cholesterol: 0 mg
Sodium: 1 mg
Fiber: trace
Exchange Approx.:
(per ⅛-c. serving):
½ Misc. Carb.

1. Dice the vegetables and layer them in a bowl with the pickling salt. Store in the refrigerator overnight to remove moisture from the vegetables.

2. Drain and rinse the vegetables. (Rinsing will remove much of the salt; however, if sodium is a concern, you can omit it altogether.)

3. To make the marinade, combine the vinegar, Splenda granular, turmeric, ginger, dried mustard, mustard seed, celery seed, and pickling spice sachet in a large, noncorrosive stockpot. Bring ingredients to a boil, and boil for 2 minutes. Add the vegetables to the stockpot and boil for an additional 10 minutes.

4. Remove the pickling spice sachet and add the pickled onions, if you are using them; boil for another 2 minutes.

5. Remove from heat and allow to cool. Pack the vegetables in jars, then fill with the pickling liquid until the vegetables are covered. Store the covered glass jars in the refrigerator. Serve chilled as a relish or on deli sandwiches.

# Pepper and Corn Relish

1. Seed and chop the peppers, and toss in a bowl with the remaining ingredients.

2. Relish can be served immediately, or chilled and served the next day. For a colorful, mild relish, use a combination of 2 tablespoons of chopped green bell pepper and an equal amount of chopped red pepper in place of the jalapeño peppers.

**Serves 4**

4 banana or jalapeño peppers
⅓ cup frozen corn, thawed
⅓ cup chopped red onion
⅛ teaspoon ground coriander
2 teaspoons lime juice
Freshly ground black pepper
    to taste

**NUTRITIONAL ANALYSIS**
(per serving):

Calories: 39
Protein: 2 g
Carbohydrate: 9 g
Fat: trace
Sat. Fat: trace
Cholesterol: 0 mg
Sodium: 7 mg
Fiber: 2 g
Exchange Approx.:
½ Starch

# Cranberry-Raisin Chutney

**Yields about 3 cups**
**Serving size: 1 tbs.**

1 cup diced onions
1 cup diced peeled apples
1 cup diced bananas
1 cup diced peaches
¼ cup raisins
¼ cup dry white wine
¼ cup dried cranberries
¼ cup apple cider vinegar
1 teaspoon honey
Sea salt and freshly ground
    black pepper to taste
    (optional)

**NUTRITIONAL ANALYSIS**
(per serving, without salt):

Calories: 13
Protein: trace
Carbohydrate: 3 g
Fat: trace
Sat. Fat: trace
Cholesterol: 0 mg
Sodium: 3 mg
Fiber: trace
Exchange Approx.:
1 Free Condiment

1. In a large saucepan, combine all the ingredients.

2. Cook over low heat for about 1 hour, stirring occasionally.

3. Cool completely. Can be kept for a week in the refrigerator or in the freezer for 3 months, or canned using the same sterilizing method you'd use to can mincemeat.

*TIP: This chutney is also good if you substitute other dried fruit for the raisins or cranberries, such as using the dried Fancy Fruit Mix (strawberries, blueberries, cranberries, sweet cherries, and tart cherries) from Nutty Guys (www .nuttyguys.com).*

# Fruit Salsa

Place all the ingredients in a food processor and process until well mixed. Do not over process; you want the salsa to remain somewhat chunky.

## Salsa Status

Salsa is now the number one condiment in America. (Source: Food Finds, *www.foodtv .com*)

**Yields about 2 cups**
**Serving size: 2 tbs.**

½ of a cantaloupe
1 jalapeño or banana pepper
1 cup blackberries
1 small red or green bell
    pepper
1 medium-sized red onion
1 tablespoon lemon juice
Optional seasonings to taste:
Parsley
Cilantro
Sea salt
Cayenne pepper

**NUTRITIONAL ANALYSIS**
(per serving):

Calories: 24
Protein: trace
Carbohydrate: 6 g
Fat: trace
Sat. Fat: trace
Cholesterol: 0 mg
Sodium: 5 mg
Fiber: 1 g
Exchange Approx.:
½ Fruit

# Marmalade-Black Bean Salsa

**Yields about 1⅛ cup**
**Serving size: 1 tbs.**

1 tablespoon sugar-free
    orange marmalade
½ cup chopped roasted red
    pepper
2 cloves roasted garlic (see
    Dry-Roasted Garlic on page
    31 for roasting instructions)
½ cup cooked black beans
1 teaspoon key lime or fresh
    lime juice
Optional seasonings to taste:
Sea salt
Freshly ground black pepper
Cilantro
Parsley

Place all the ingredients in a food processor and process until well mixed. Do not over process; you want the salsa to remain somewhat chunky.

**NUTRITIONAL ANALYSIS**
(per serving):

Calories: 8
Protein: trace
Carbohydrate: 2 g
Fat: trace
Sat. Fat: trace
Cholesterol: 0 mg
Sodium: trace mg
Fiber: 1 g
Exchange Approx.:
1 Free Condiment

# Strawberry Spoon Sweet

1. Combine all the ingredients in a large bowl. Microwave uncovered on high for 3 to 5 minutes, or until the liquid thickens a little.

2. Remove and discard the thyme sprigs. Let cool, then refrigerate for several hours to set before serving. This recipe keeps for several months in the refrigerator.

**Yields 1 quart**
**Serving size: 2 tbs.**

6 cups small, hulled
   strawberries
¾ cup Splenda granular
½ cup dry red wine
5–7 fresh thyme sprigs

**NUTRITIONAL ANALYSIS**
(per serving):

Calories: 15
Protein: trace
Carbohydrate: 3 g
Fat: trace
Sat. Fat: trace
Cholesterol: 0 mg
Sodium: 3 mg
Fiber: 1 g
Exchange Approx.:
½ Fruit, ¼ Misc. Carb.

# Pineapple-Chili Salsa

**Serves 4**

½ cup unsweetened, diced
  pineapple
½ cup roughly chopped
  papaya, peach, or mango
1 small poblano chili pepper
¼ cup chopped red bell
  pepper
¼ cup chopped yellow bell
  pepper
1 tablespoon fresh key lime or
  fresh lime juice
¼ cup chopped red onion

**NUTRITIONAL ANALYSIS**
(per serving):

Calories: 29
Protein: 1 g
Carbohydrate: 7 g
Fat: trace
Sat. Fat: trace
Cholesterol: 0 mg
Sodium: 2 mg
Fiber: 1 g
Exchange Approx.:
½ Fruit

Combine all the ingredients in a bowl and toss to mix.

# Salsa with a Kick

Place all the ingredients in a blender or food processor; process briefly, until blended but not smooth.

**Yields about 2 cups**
**Serving size: 1 tbs.**

2 teaspoons ground flaxseed
4 medium tomatoes, chopped
1 clove garlic, chopped
½ of a small onion
½ tablespoon cider vinegar
¼ teaspoon Tabasco sauce
⅛ teaspoon ground cayenne
   pepper
1 tablespoon chopped fresh
   coriander

**NUTRITIONAL ANALYSIS**
(per serving):

Calories: 5
Protein: trace
Carbohydrate: 1 g
Fat: trace
Sat. Fat: trace
Cholesterol: 0 mg
Sodium: 2 mg
Fiber: trace
Exchange Approx.:
3 tbs. = 1 Free Condi-
ment

# Avocado-Corn Salsa

**Serves 4**

1 cup corn kernels, blanched fresh or thawed frozen
1 small banana pepper, seeded and chopped
¼ cup diced red radishes
⅛ cup thinly sliced green onion
1 avocado, diced
1 tablespoon lime juice
½ teaspoon white wine vinegar
1 teaspoon extra-virgin olive oil
¼ teaspoon dried oregano
Dash of ground cumin
Dash of Tabasco sauce
Freshly ground black pepper (optional)

1. Combine the corn, banana pepper, radish, and green onion in a medium bowl.

2. In another bowl, combine half of the diced avocado and the lime juice, and stir to thoroughly coat.

3. In a blender, combine the other half of the avocado, the vinegar, oil, oregano, cumin, and Tabasco.

4. Process until smooth, then pour it over the corn mixture and stir. Add the avocado mixture. Serve immediately.

---

**NUTRITIONAL ANALYSIS**
(per serving):

Calories: 133
Protein: 2 g
Carbohydrate: 14 g
Fat: 9 g
Sat. Fat: 1 g
Cholesterol: 0 mg
Sodium: 10 mg
Fiber: 4 g
Exchange Approx.:
½ Starch/Vegetable,
2 Fats

# Blackberry Sauce

1. Heat the blackberry preserves in a small saucepan over medium heat until melted. Stir in remaining ingredients.

2. Bring the mixture to a boil, lower the heat, and simmer for 1 minute, stirring constantly. Use the cooled sauce as a meat seasoning, or as a dip for eggrolls.

## Dipping Sauce

Whisk together: 1 tablespoon rice wine vinegar, 2½ teaspoons water, 2 teaspoons sesame oil, 2 teaspoons minced scallions or green onions, and ⅛ teaspoon Splenda granular. Use with pot stickers, steamed dumplings, or egg rolls. A 2-teaspoon serving has: Calories: 21; Protein: trace g; Carbohydrate: trace g; Fat: 2 g; Sat. Fat: trace g; Cholesterol: 0 mg; Sodium: trace mg; Fiber: trace g; Exchange Approximations: ½ Fat.

**Yields 1¼ cups**
**Serving size: 1 tbs.**

1 cup sugar-free blackberry preserves
2 teaspoons grated lemon zest
1 tablespoon lemon juice
1 tablespoon rice wine vinegar
½ teaspoon ground ginger
½ teaspoon crushed anise seeds
¼ teaspoon dry mustard
¼ teaspoon ground cinnamon
⅛ teaspoon ground cloves
⅛ teaspoon hot pepper sauce

**NUTRITIONAL ANALYSIS**
(per serving):

Calories: 9
Protein: trace
Carbohydrate: 4 g
Fat: trace
Sat. Fat: trace
Cholesterol: 0 mg
Sodium: 1 mg
Fiber: trace
Exchange Approx.:
½ Fruit

# Roasted Red Pepper and Plum Sauce

**Yields 2 cups**
**Serving size: 1 tbs.**

1 large roasted red pepper (pulp only)
½ pound apricots, quartered and pitted
¾ pound plums, quartered and pitted
1⅓ cups apple cider vinegar
⅔ cup water
¼ cup Splenda granular
2 tablespoons of honey
2 tablespoons fresh grated ginger
1 teaspoon salt
1 tablespoon toasted mustard seeds
4 scallions, chopped (white part only)
1 teaspoon minced garlic
½ teaspoon ground cinnamon

---

**NUTRITIONAL ANALYSIS**
(per serving):

Calories: 19
Protein: trace
Carbohydrate: 5 g
Fat: trace
Sat. Fat: trace
Cholesterol: 0 mg
Sodium: 75 mg
Fiber: 1 g
Exchange Approx.:
½ Misc. Carb.

1. Place all the ingredients together in a large pot and bring to a boil. Reduce heat and simmer, covered, for 30 minutes.

2. Uncover and simmer for another hour. Place in a blender or food processor and process to desired consistency. Can be stored in refrigerator for 4 to 6 weeks.

## Speedy Sauce

In a hurry? You can make an individual "1 Fruit"-choice blackberry sauce by mixing 1 tablespoon of sugar-free blackberry preserves, ⅛ teaspoon white wine vinegar or rice wine vinegar, ⅛ teaspoon Bragg's Liquid Aminos or low-sodium soy sauce, and some seasonings (such as a pinch of dried onion, minced garlic, ground ginger, allspice, and cayenne or crushed red pepper flakes). Mix together the ingredients in a microwave-safe cup and heat until mixture comes to a boil. Add pinch of cornstarch and whisk until it stops boiling, then serve.

# Homemade Worcestershire Sauce

1. Combine all the ingredients in large saucepan. Stir over heat until the mixture boils.

2. Lower the heat and simmer uncovered for 1 hour, stirring occasionally. Store in a covered jar in the refrigerator.

## Mock Hollandaise Sauce

Mix ⅛ cup yogurt with 1 teaspoon lemon juice, and serve with Eggs Benedict Redux (see page 53). The Nutritional Analysis for a 2-tablespoon serving is: Calories: 17; Protein: 2 g; Carbohydrate: 3 g; Fat: 1 g; Sat. Fat: trace g; Cholesterol: 1 mg; Sodium: 22 mg; Fiber: trace g. Exchange Approximations: 1 Free.

**Yields 1 cup**
**Serving size: 1 tbs.**

1½ cups cider vinegar
¼ cup sugar-free blackberry preserves
1 tablespoon sugar-free maple-flavored syrup
1 clove garlic, crushed
⅛ teaspoon chili powder
⅛ teaspoon ground cloves
Pinch of cayenne pepper
¼ cup chopped onion
½ teaspoon ground allspice
⅛ teaspoon dry mustard
1 teaspoon Bragg's Liquid Aminos

**NUTRITIONAL ANALYSIS**
(per serving):

Calories: 8
Protein: trace
Carbohydrate: 3 g
Fat: trace
Sat. Fat: trace
Cholesterol: 0 mg
Sodium: 20 mg
Fiber: trace
Exchange Approx.:
1 Free Condiment

# Pesto Sauce

**Yields about 3 cups**
**Serving size: 1 tbs.**

¾ cup pine nuts
4 cups tightly packed basil
   leaves
½ cup freshly grated
   Parmesan cheese
3 large garlic cloves, minced
¼ teaspoon salt
1 teaspoon freshly ground
   black pepper
½ cup extra-virgin olive oil

---

**NUTRITIONAL ANALYSIS**
(per serving):

Calories: 37
Protein: 1 g
Carbohydrate: 1 g
Fat: 4 g
Sat. Fat: 1 g
Cholesterol: 1 mg
Sodium: 14 mg
Fiber: trace
Exchange Approx.:
1 Fat

1. Preheat oven to 350°F. Spread the pine nuts on a baking sheet and bake for about 5 minutes; stir the nuts. Continue to bake until the nuts are golden brown and highly aromatic, stirring occasionally. Let the nuts cool completely, then chop finely.

2. Fill a medium-sized heavy saucepan halfway with water. Place over medium heat and bring the water to a boil. Next to the pot, place a large bowl filled with water and ice. Using tongs, dip a few of the basil leaves into the boiling water, blanch for 3 seconds, then quickly remove them from the boiling water and place them in the ice water. Repeat process until all of the basil has been blanched, adding ice to the water as needed. Drain the basil in a colander and pat dry with a towel.

3. In a blender or food processor, combine the basil, pine nuts, cheese, garlic, salt, pepper, and all but 1 tablespoon of the olive oil; process until the pesto is smooth and uniform. Pour the pesto into an airtight container and add the remaining olive oil to the top to act as a protective barrier. Pesto can be stored in the refrigerator for up to 5 days.

4. To freeze pesto, place it in a tightly sealed container. To freeze small amounts of pesto to use in recipes, pour the pesto into ice cube trays and freeze until solid. Once it's frozen, you can remove the pesto cubes and place them in sealed freezer bags.

## Preserving Fresh Basil

If you have a large crop of fresh basil, blanch and freeze it in ice cubes for easy-to-use portions. Follow the instructions for blanching the basil in the Pesto Sauce recipe on this page.

# Gingered Peach Sauce

1. Heat the olive oil in a nonstick skillet over medium heat and sauté the shallot and ginger. Add the wine and simmer until reduced by half. Add the diced peach, orange juice concentrate, and Bragg's Liquid Aminos; return to a simmer, stirring occasionally.

2. In a separate container, mix the cornstarch with a tablespoon of the sauce; stir to create a slurry, mixing well to remove any lumps. Add the slurry to the sauce and simmer until the mixture thickens. Transfer the mixture to a blender or food processor and process until smooth.

**Serves 4**

2 teaspoons olive oil
1 tablespoon chopped shallot
2 teaspoons grated fresh ginger
⅓ cup dry white wine
1 small peach, peeled and diced
1 tablespoon frozen unsweetened orange juice concentrate
1 teaspoon Bragg's Liquid Aminos
½ teaspoon cornstarch

**NUTRITIONAL ANALYSIS**
(per serving):

Calories: 54
Protein: 1 g
Carbohydrate: 5 g
Fat: 2 g
Sat. Fat: trace
Cholesterol: 0 mg
Sodium: 57 mg
Fiber: trace
Exchange Approx.:
½ Fat, 1 Fruit

# Mock Cream

**Yields 1¼ cups**

1 cup skim milk
¼ cup nonfat dry milk

---

**NUTRITIONAL ANALYSIS**
(per recipe):

Calories: 147
Protein: 14 g
Carbohydrate: 21 g
Fat: 1 g
Sat. Fat: trace
Cholesterol: 8 mg
Sodium: 221 mg
Fiber: 0 g
Exchange Approx.:
1½ Skim Milks

Process the ingredients in a blender until mixed, and use as a substitute for heavy cream.

## Comparative Analysis

Using 1¼ cups heavy cream would give you the following breakdown: Calories: 515; Protein: 3 g; Carbohydrate: 4 g; Fat: 55 g; Sat. Fat: 34 g; Cholesterol: 205 mg; Sodium: 56 mg; Fiber: 0 g; PCF Ratio: 2-3-95. Exchange Approximations: 11 Fat.

# Mock White Sauce

1. In a medium-sized, heavy nonstick saucepan, melt the butter over very low heat. The butter should gently melt; you do not want it to bubble and turn brown. While the butter is melting, mix together the flour, salt, and white pepper in a small bowl.

2. Once the butter is melted, add the flour mixture to the butter and stir constantly. (A heat-safe, flat-bottom spoon safe for nonstick pans works well for this.) Once the mixture thickens and starts to bubble, slowly pour in some of the Mock Cream. Stir until it's blended in with the roux.

3. Add a little more of the Mock Cream and stir until blended. Add the remaining Mock Cream and continue cooking, stirring constantly to make sure the sauce doesn't stick to the bottom of the pan.

4. Once the sauce begins to steam and appears it's just about to boil, reduce the heat and simmer until the sauce thickens, or about 3 minutes.

## Mock Sour Cream

In a blender, combine: ⅛ cup nonfat yogurt, ¼ cup nonfat cottage cheese, and ½ teaspoon vinegar. If you prefer a more sour taste, add another ½ teaspoon of vinegar. The type of vinegar you use will affect the taste as well. Apple cider vinegar tends to be more sour than white wine vinegar, for example. The Nutritional Analysis for each tablespoon is: Calories: 8; Protein: 1 g; Carbohydrate: 1 g; Fat: trace g; Sat. Fat: trace g; Cholesterol: trace mg; Sodium: 4 mg; Fiber: 0 g; PCF Ratio: 70-26-4. Exchange Approximations: ½ Free.

**Yields about 1 cup**
**Serving size:** ½ **cup**

1 tablespoon unsalted butter
1 tablespoon flour
¼ teaspoon sea salt
Pinch of white pepper
1 cup Mock Cream (see recipe on page 20)

---

**NUTRITIONAL ANALYSIS**
(per recipe):

Calories: 61
Protein: 3 g
Carbohydrate: 6 g
Fat: 3 g
Sat. Fat: 2 g
Cholesterol: 9 mg
Sodium: 190 mg
Fiber: trace
Exchange Approx.:
½ Fat, ½ Skim Milk

# Fat-Free Roux

**Yields enough to thicken 1 cup of liquid**
**Serving size:** ¼ cup

1 tablespoon cornstarch
2 tablespoons wine

**NUTRITIONAL ANALYSIS**
(per serving, roux only):

Calories: 13
Protein: trace
Carbohydrate: 2 g
Fat: 0 g
Sat. Fat: 0 g
Cholesterol: 0 mg
Sodium: 1 mg
Fiber: trace
Exchange Approx.:
1 Free

1. Make this roux with red wine for a defatted beef broth gravy. Use white wine if you plan to use it for chicken or seafood gravy or sauce. Whisk ingredients together until well-blended, making sure there are no lumps.

2. To use as a thickener for 1 cup of broth, heat the broth until it reaches a boil. Slowly whisk the cornstarch-wine mixture into the broth and return to a boil, then reduce heat; simmer, stirring constantly, until the mixture thickens enough to coat the back of a spoon. (A gravy or sauce made in this manner will thicken more as it cools. It's important to bring a cornstarch slurry to a boil; this helps it thicken and removes the "starchy" taste.)

## Flavor Facts

Regardless of the thickener you use to make gravy, be sure to strain the pan drippings to remove as much residue fat as possible. That way you'll save the juice—and flavor—of the meat.

# Madeira Sauce

1. Heat the olive oil in a nonstick saucepan over medium heat.

2. Add the garlic and shallot, and sauté until translucent. Add the tomato paste and sauté for 30 seconds, stirring as needed. Add the Madeira, broth, lemon juice, Mock Cream, and simmer until the mixture is reduced by half.

3. Whisk in the butter to form an emulsion. Optional: Strain the sauce and season with salt and pepper.

*TIP: Keep the sauce warm until needed, being careful not to let it boil or become too cold after the butter has been added.*

**Serves 4**

2 teaspoons olive oil
1 clove garlic, crushed
1 tablespoon chopped shallot
1 teaspoon unsalted tomato paste
⅓ cup Madeira
¼ cup shellfish, vegetable, or chicken broth
1 tablespoon lemon juice
2 teaspoons Mock Cream (see page 20)
2 teaspoons unsalted butter
Salt and freshly ground black pepper (optional)

**NUTRITIONAL ANALYSIS**
(per serving):

Calories: 56
Protein: trace
Carbohydrate: 2 g
Fat: 4 g
Sat. Fat: 2 g
Cholesterol: 5 mg
Sodium: 3 mg
Fiber: trace
Exchange Approx.:
1 Fat, ½ Vegetable

# Mock Béchamel Sauce

**Yields 1 cup**
**Serving size:** ¼ **cup**

1 egg
1 cup Mock Cream (see page
  20)
1 teaspoon unsalted butter

---

**NUTRITIONAL ANALYSIS**
(per serving):

Calories: 53
Protein: 4 g
Carbohydrate: 4 g
Fat: 2 g
Sat. Fat: 1 g
Cholesterol: 51 mg
Sodium: 58 mg
Fiber: 0 g
Exchange Approx.:
½ Fat, ½ Skim Milk

1. In a quart-size or larger microwave-safe bowl, whisk the egg into the Mock Cream until it's well blended. Microwave on high for 1 minute. Whisk the mixture again. Microwave on high for 30 seconds and then whisk the mixture again. Microwave on high for another 30 seconds, then whisk again. (Strain the mixture if there appears to be any cooked egg solids; this seldom occurs if the mixture is whisked at the intervals specified.)

2. Allow the mixture to cool slightly, then whisk in the butter.

# Mock Cauliflower Sauce

1. Add the cauliflower, onion, garlic, and white wine to a microwave-safe bowl. Cover and microwave on high for 5 minutes, or until the cauliflower is tender and the onions are transparent. (Microwave on high for additional 1-minute intervals, if necessary.)

2. Pour the vegetable-wine mixture into a blender or food processor container, being careful not to burn yourself on the steam. Season with the white pepper, add the Mock Cream, and process until smooth.

*TIP: If you use frozen cauliflower to make Mock Cauliflower Sauce, be sure to thaw and drain it first. Otherwise, there will be too much moisture and the resulting sauce will be too thin.*

**Serves 4**

2 cups cauliflower
¼ cup diced Spanish onion
1 tablespoon dry white wine
⅛ cup (2 tablespoons) Mock Cream (see page 20)
½ clove roasted garlic or ½ clove crushed garlic
Freshly ground white pepper to taste

**NUTRITIONAL ANALYSIS**
(per serving):

Calories: 27
Protein: 2 g
Carbohydrate: 5 g
Fat: trace
Sat. Fat: trace
Cholesterol: trace
Sodium: 16 mg
Fiber: 2 g
Exchange Approx.:
1 Vegetable

# Appetizers

## chapter two

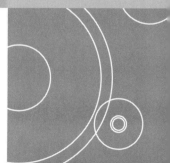

# Cucumber Slices with Smoked Salmon Cream

**Yields about ½ cup**
**Serving size: 1 tsp.**

2–3 cucumbers
1 ounce Ducktrap River
  smoked salmon
8 ounces Neufchâtel cheese,
  room temperature
½ tablespoon lemon juice
½ teaspoon freshly ground
  pepper
Dried dill (optional)

## NUTRITIONAL ANALYSIS
(per serving):

Calories: 27
Protein: 1 g
Carbohydrate: 1 g
Fat: 2 g
Sat. Fat: 1 g
Cholesterol: 7 mg
Sodium: 50 mg
Fiber: 0 g
Exchange Approx.:
½ Fat

1. Cut the cucumbers into slices about ¼-inch thick. Place the slices on paper towels to drain while you prepare the salmon cream.

2. Combine the smoked salmon, Neufchâtel cheese, lemon juice, and pepper in a food processor; blend until smooth.

3. Fit a pastry bag with your choice of tip, and spoon the salmon cream into the bag. Pipe 1 teaspoon of the salmon cream atop each cucumber slice. Garnish with dried dill, if desired.

## Comparative Analysis

If you choose to use cream cheese instead of Neufchâtel, the Nutritional Analysis will be: Calories: 35; Protein: 1 g; Carbohydrate: 1 g; Fat: 3 g; Sat. Fat: 2 g; Cholesterol: 10 mg; Sodium: 41 mg; Fiber: 1 g; PCF Ratio: 11-6-84. Exchange Approximations: 1 Fat.

# Flaxseed Oil–Fortified Salsa Dip

Blend all the ingredients together in food processor or blender for a smooth dip; otherwise, mix thoroughly with a fork.

## Preventative Measures

Whole ground flaxseed is rich in phyto-estrogens (the plant substances that mimic the female sex hormone estrogen) in even greater quantities than in soy, so it's now also considered another possible way to help prevent breast cancer in postmenopausal women. Flaxseed also has omega-3 and -6 essential fatty acids, both of which are known for their health benefits. (Source: WebMDHealth, *http://my.webmd.com*)

**Yields about 1 cup**
**Serving size: 1 tbs.**

⅛ cup flaxseed oil
½ cup mild salsa
1 teaspoon freeze-dried chives
1 teaspoon dried basil
Pinch of sea salt
¼ cup chopped onion

**NUTRITIONAL ANALYSIS**
(per serving):

Calories: 18
Protein: trace
Carbohydrate: 1 g
Fat: 2 g
Sat. Fat: trace
Cholesterol: 0 mg
Sodium: 49 mg
Fiber: trace
Exchange Approx.:
3 servings = 1 Fat

# Lemon Tahini Vegetable Dip

**Yields about 5 cups**
**Serving size: 1 tbs.**

1 cup sesame seeds
¼ cup lemon juice
1 cup water
2 tablespoons ground
    flaxseed
1 teaspoon garlic powder
⅛ teaspoon cider vinegar
1 teaspoon sea salt

**NUTRITIONAL ANALYSIS**
(per serving):

Calories: 26
Protein: 1 g
Carbohydrate: 1 g
Fat: 2 g
Sat. Fat: trace
Cholesterol: 0 mg
Sodium: 61 mg
Fiber: 2 g
Exchange Approx.:
½ Fat

Put all the ingredients in a food processor and blend until smooth.

# Garlic and Feta Cheese Dip

1. In a food processor, combine all the ingredients and process until thoroughly mixed.

2. Cover and chill until ready to serve with assorted vegetables. This dip is somewhat high in fat if you use regular cream cheese, whereas nonfat cream cheese would lower the total fat in this recipe by 38 grams. People on a salt-restricted diet need to check with their dietitians about using nonfat cream cheese because it's much higher in sodium.

## Dry-Roasted Garlic

Roasted garlic is delicious spread on toasted baguette slices, but is also flavorful in some of the salad dressings and other recipes in this book. The traditional method calls for roasting a full head of garlic in olive oil. Dry roasting works just as well and doesn't add fat. Preheat oven to 350°F and lightly spray a small, covered baking dish with nonstick spray. Slice off ½ inch from the top of each garlic head and rub off any loose skins, being careful not to separate the cloves. Place the garlic in baking dish, cut-side up (if roasting more than 1 head of garlic, arrange them in the dish so that they don't touch). Cover and bake until the garlic cloves are very tender when pierced, about 30 to 45 minutes. Roasted garlic heads will keep in the refrigerator for 2 or 3 days.

**Yields 1½ cups**
**Serving size: 1 tbs.**

½ cup feta cheese, crumbled
4 ounces softened cream cheese
¼ cup Hellmann's or Best Foods Real Mayonnaise
1 clove dry-roasted garlic (see Dry Roasted Garlic on this page)
¼ teaspoon dried basil
¼ teaspoon dried cilantro or oregano
⅛ teaspoon dried dill
⅛ teaspoon dried thyme

**NUTRITIONAL ANALYSIS**
(per serving):

Calories: 11
Protein: trace
Carbohydrate: trace
Fat: 1 g
Sat. Fat: 1 g
Cholesterol: 0 mg
Sodium: 22 mg
Fiber: 0 g
Exchange Approx.:
1 Free

# Spicy Almond Dip

**Yields about ½ cup**
**Serving size: 1 tbs.**

¼ cup ground, raw almonds
2 teaspoons Worcestershire
  sauce (see recipe for
  Homemade Worcestershire
  on page 17)
½ teaspoon honey
½ teaspoon chili powder
1 teaspoon poppy seeds
½ teaspoon onion powder
⅛ cup water
Pinch of black pepper

**NUTRITIONAL ANALYSIS**
(per serving):

Calories: 23
Protein: 1 g
Carbohydrate: 1 g
Fat: 2 g
Sat. Fat: trace
Cholesterol: 0 mg
Sodium: 18 mg
Fiber: trace
Exchange Approx.:
½ Fat

Put all the ingredients in a food processor and blend until smooth.

# Cinnamon Nut Butter

1. Put all the ingredients in a food processor and blend to desired consistency, scraping down the sides of the bowl as necessary.

2. Serve with toast points, crackers, or celery sticks. Refrigerate any leftovers.

**Yields ¾ cup**
**Serving size: 1 tsp.**

¼ cup sesame seeds
¼ cup ground almonds
¼ cup sunflower seeds
1 tablespoon honey
½ teaspoon cinnamon
Pinch of unsweetened cocoa
    (optional)
Pinch of sea salt (optional)

**NUTRITIONAL ANALYSIS**
(per serving):

Calories: 19
Protein: 1 g
Carbohydrate: 1 g
Fat: 2 g
Sat. Fat: trace
Cholesterol: 0 mg
Sodium: 4 mg
Fiber: trace
Exchange Approx.:
½ Fat

# Onion Dip

**Yields 1½ cups**
**Serving size: 1 tbs.**

1 cup nonfat yogurt
1 tablespoon olive oil
½ cup water
1 teaspoon lemon juice
1 teaspoon cider vinegar
1 medium-sized sweet onion,
    chopped
Sea salt to taste (optional)
Lemon pepper to taste
    (optional)

---

**NUTRITIONAL ANALYSIS**
(per serving, without salt):

Calories: 12
Protein: 1 g
Carbohydrate: 1 g
Fat: 1 g
Sat. Fat: trace
Cholesterol: trace
Sodium: 7 mg
Fiber: trace
Exchange Approx.:
1 Free Condiment

Combine all the ingredients in a food processor and pulse to desired consistency. Refrigerate for 1 hour to allow the flavors to merge, then serve.

## Quick Thickener

If your dip or spread is too runny, stir in ¼ teaspoon of potato flour. Let it set for 1 or 2 minutes, then add more flour if necessary. The addition of potato flour won't make a significant change to the flavor or Exchange Approximations.

# French Onion Soup Dip

1. Put the onion and beef broth in a microwave-safe dish. Cover and microwave on high for 1 minute; stir. Continue to microwave on high for 30-second intervals until the onion is transparent. Stir in Parmesan cheese. Set aside and allow to cool.

2. In a blender, process the cottage cheese until smooth. Mix the cottage cheese into the onion mixture. Serve warm or refrigerate until needed and serve cold.

## Guilt-Free Flavors

Adjust the flavor of dips or spreads without adding calories by adding onion or garlic powder or your choice of herbs.

**Yields about 1¾ cups**
**Serving size: 1 tbs.**

1 cup chopped sweet onion
2 tablespoons reduced double-strength beef broth (boiled for a richer broth)
1 tablespoon Parmesan cheese
1 cup nonfat cottage cheese

---

**NUTRITIONAL ANALYSIS**
(per serving):

Calories: 7
Protein: 1 g
Carbohydrate: trace
Fat: trace
Sat. Fat: trace
Cholesterol: trace
Sodium: 11 mg
Fiber: trace
Exchange Approx.:
1 Free Condiment

# Horseradish Dip

**Yields 1¾ cups**
**Serving size: 1 tbs.**

1 cup nonfat cottage cheese
1 tablespoon olive oil
½ cup nonfat plain yogurt
3 tablespoons prepared
    horseradish
1 teaspoon lemon juice
Optional seasonings to taste:
Onion powder
Cumin
Sea salt
Ginger

**NUTRITIONAL ANALYSIS**
(per serving):

Calories: 12
Protein: 1 g
Carbohydrate: 1 g
Fat: 1 g
Sat. Fat: trace
Cholesterol: 0 mg
Sodium: 9 mg
Fiber: trace
Exchange Approx.:
1 Free Condiment

Combine all the ingredients in a blender or food processor and process until smooth.

# Bean Dip

Add the beans, Liquid Aminos, cider vinegar, honey, and dried herbs to a blender, and process until smooth. Stir in remaining ingredients.

## Low-Sodium Substitutions

Bragg's Liquid Aminos is a lower-sodium substitution for soy sauce. Because Bragg's isn't a fermented product, many people who can't tolerate soy can use it.

**Yields about 2 cups**
**Serving size: 1 tbs.**

½ cup cooked pinto (or other) beans
1 tablespoon Bragg's Liquid Aminos
3 tablespoons cider vinegar
1 teaspoon honey
¼ teaspoon dried basil
¼ teaspoon dried parsley
1 stalk celery, diced
¼ cup chopped green onion
½ cup alfalfa sprouts, lightly chopped
1 medium tomato, diced

---

**NUTRITIONAL ANALYSIS**
(per serving):

Calories: 7
Protein: trace
Carbohydrate: 1 g
Fat: trace
Sat. Fat: trace
Cholesterol: 0 mg
Sodium: 23 mg
Fiber: trace
Exchange Approx.:
½ Free Condiment

# Garbanzo Dip

**Yields about 2 cups**
**Serving size: 1 tbs.**

3 cups cooked garbanzo (or
   other) white beans
½ teaspoon ground cumin
1 tablespoon lemon juice
1 tablespoon parsley flakes
¼ teaspoon dried basil
1 teaspoon onion powder
¼ teaspoon garlic powder
1 tablespoon honey

**NUTRITIONAL ANALYSIS**
(per serving):

Calories: 25
Protein: 2 g
Carbohydrate: 5 g
Fat: trace
Sat. Fat: trace
Cholesterol: 0 mg
Sodium: 1 mg
Fiber: 1 g
Exchange Approx.:
½ Very Lean Meat

Combine all the ingredients in a food processor or blender and process until smooth. Add
a teaspoon of water or bean broth if you need
to thin the dip.

# Herbed Cheese Spread

Place the herbs in a food processor and pulse until chopped. Add the cheeses and process until smooth.

## Toasted Nut Garnish

Herbed Cheese Spread is good on Garlic Toast (see page 127) sprinkled with a few toasted pine nuts, sunflower or sesame seeds, or other chopped nuts. Toast the nuts in a small skillet in a single layer. Over low heat, toast until lightly golden, stirring often to prevent burning. This takes 3 or 4 minutes. Cool on paper towels.

**Yields about 1 cup**
**Serving size: 1 tbs.**

2 teaspoons chopped fresh parsley leaves
2 teaspoons chopped fresh chives
1 teaspoon chopped fresh thyme
½ cup nonfat cottage cheese
½ teaspoon freshly ground black pepper
4 ounces Neufchâtel cheese, at room temperature

### NUTRITIONAL ANALYSIS
(per serving):

Calories: 20
Protein: 1 g
Carbohydrate: trace
Fat: 2 g
Sat. Fat: 1 g
Cholesterol: 5 mg
Sodium: 26 mg
Fiber: trace
Exchange Approx.:
¼ Skim Milk or 1 Free
Condiment

# Zesty Almond Spread

**Yields about ¼ cup**
**Serving size: 1 tbs.**

30 unsalted almonds
2 teaspoons honey
1 teaspoon chili powder
¼ teaspoon garlic powder
Pinch of sea salt (optional)

**NUTRITIONAL ANALYSIS**
(per serving, without salt):

Calories: 50
Protein: 2 g
Carbohydrate: 4 g
Fat: 4 g
Sat. Fat: trace
Cholesterol: 0 mg
Sodium: trace mg
Fiber: trace
Exchange Approx.:
1 Fat

Place all the ingredients in a food processor or blender and process to desired consistency.

# Almond Honey Mustard

Add all the ingredients to a food processor or blender and process until smooth.

**Yields about ½ cup**
**Serving size: 1 tsp.**

¼ cup unsalted almond butter
2 teaspoons mustard
1 teaspoon honey
2 tablespoons lemon juice
½ teaspoon garlic powder
Pinch of cumin (optional)
Pinch of sea salt (optional)

**NUTRITIONAL ANALYSIS**
(per serving, without salt):

Calories: 21
Protein: trace
Carbohydrate: 1 g
Fat: 2 g
Sat. Fat: trace
Cholesterol: 0 mg
Sodium: 6 mg
Fiber: trace
Exchange Approx.:
½ Fat

# Smoked Mussel Spread

**Yields 4¼ cup**
**Serving size: 1 tbs.**

4 ounces cream cheese
1 cup nonfat plain yogurt
½ cup nonfat cottage cheese
2 ounces Ducktrap River
   smoked mussels
¼ cup chopped onion or
   scallion
1 teaspoon dried dill
1 teaspoon dried parsley

---

**NUTRITIONAL ANALYSIS**
(per serving):

Calories: 21
Protein: 1 g
Carbohydrate: 1 g
Fat: 1 g
Sat. Fat: trace
Cholesterol: 5 mg
Sodium: 30 mg
Fiber: trace
Exchange Approx.:
½ Fat

1. Place all the ingredients in a food processor or blender and process until smooth.

2. Chill for at least 2 hours or overnight before serving. This spread also works well made with smoked oysters, shrimp, or turkey. Serve on crackers or cracker-sized bread rounds.

## Conservative Exchanges

Keep in mind that whenever Exchange Approximations are given in this book, it's always with an "err on the side of caution" philosophy, so the numbers are rounded up.

# Easy Olive Spread

1. Combine the olives, garlic, herbs, and spices in a food processor and pulse until chopped. Transfer to a bowl and set aside.

2. Add the cottage cheese, cream cheese, and mayonnaise to the blender or food processor and process until smooth. Fold the cheese mixture into the chopped olive mixture.

## Delicious Substitutions

Substitute marinated mushrooms or artichoke hearts for the olives in the Easy Olive Spread recipe.

**Yields about 3 cups**
**Serving size: 1 tbs.**

1 cup black olives
3 cloves garlic
1 tablespoon fresh Italian flat-
    leaf parsley
1 tablespoon fresh basil
2 teaspoons minced lemon
    zest
Freshly ground black pepper
    to taste
½ cup nonfat cottage cheese
2 tablespoons cream cheese
1 tablespoon Hellmann's
    or Best Foods Real
    Mayonnaise

**NUTRITIONAL ANALYSIS**
(per serving):

Calories: 15
Protein: 1 g
Carbohydrate: 1 g
Fat: 1 g
Sat. Fat: trace
Cholesterol: 1 mg
Sodium: 56 mg
Fiber: trace
Exchange Approx.:
1 Free Condiment

# Mushroom Caviar

**Yields about 3 cups**
**Serving size: 1 tbs.**

1½ cups portobello
  mushrooms
1½ cups white button
  mushrooms
¼ cup chopped scallions
4 cloves dry-roasted garlic
  (see Dry-Roasted Garlic
  on page 31)
1 teaspoon fresh lemon juice
½ teaspoon balsamic vinegar
1 tablespoon extra-virgin
  olive oil
½ teaspoon fresh, chopped
  thyme (optional)
Sea salt and freshly ground
  black pepper to taste
  (optional)

1. Cut the portobello mushrooms into ¼-inch cubes. Cut the white button mushrooms into halves or quarters. (The mushroom pieces should be roughly uniform in size.) Place the mushrooms and chopped scallion in a microwave-safe bowl; cover, and microwave on high for 1 minute. Rotate the bowl. Microwave for 30-second intervals until tender.

2. Transfer the scallions and mushrooms to a food processor. (Reserve any liquid to use for thinning the "caviar," if necessary.) Pulse the food processor several times to chop the mixture, scraping down the sides of the bowl as needed. Add the remaining ingredients and pulse until mixed. Place in a small crock or serving bowl, and serve warm.

## Pseudo-Sauté

When onions and scallions are sautéed in butter or oil, they go through a caramelization process that doesn't occur when they're steamed. To create this flavor without increasing the fat in a recipe, transfer steamed vegetables to a nonstick wok or skillet (coated with nonstick spray, or a small portion of the oil called for in the recipe) and sauté until the extra moisture evaporates.

# Gluten-Free Sesame Seed Crackers

1. Preheat oven to 400°F. Mix together all ingredients, then add the water, a little at a time, to form a soft doughlike consistency. Be careful not to work the dough too much; you do not want to knead spelt flour.

2. On a floured surface, use a rolling pin to roll the dough until it's ⅛-inch thick. Use a cookie cutter to cut it into shapes and place them on a cookie sheet treated with nonstick spray. (Or use a pizza cutter to crosscut the dough into square- or rectangular-shaped crackers.) Prick each cracker with a fork. Bake for about 12 minutes or until golden brown. Store cooled crackers in an airtight container.

**Yields 36 crackers**
**Serving size: 1 cracker**

1½ cups spelt flour
1 cup sesame seeds
¼ cup arrowroot
1 tablespoons olive or
    vegetable oil
3 tablespoons nonfat yogurt
¼ cup nonfat dry milk
½ teaspoon Ener-G
    nonaluminum baking
    powder
½ cup water
⅔ teaspoon sea salt (optional)

**NUTRITIONAL ANALYSIS**
(per serving):

Calories: 50
Protein: 2 g
Carbohydrate: 5 g
Fat: 3 g
Sat. Fat: trace
Cholesterol: trace
Sodium: 5 mg
Fiber: 1 g
Exchange Approx.:
½ Starch

# Breakfast Foods

## chapter three

# Egg White Pancakes

## Serves 2

4 egg whites
½ cup oatmeal
4 teaspoons sugar-free
   strawberry jam

### NUTRITIONAL ANALYSIS
(per serving):

Calories: 113
Protein: 10 g
Carbohydrate: 18 g
Fat: 8 g
Sat. Fat: trace
Cholesterol: 0 mg
Sodium: 113 mg
Fiber: 2 g
Exchange Approx.:
1 Free Sweet, 1 Lean
Meat, 1½ Breads

1. Put all the ingredients in a blender and process until smooth.

2. Preheat a nonstick pan treated with cooking spray over medium heat. Pour half of the mixture into the pan and cook for 4 to 5 minutes.

3. Flip the pancake and cook until the inside of the cake is cooked. Repeat using remaining batter for second pancake.

## Creative Toppings

Experiment with toast and pancake toppings. Try a tablespoon of raisins, almonds, apples, bananas, berries, nut butters (limit these to 1 teaspoon per serving), peanuts, pears, walnuts, or wheat germ.

# Buckwheat Pancakes

1. Sift the flours and baking powder together. Combine the egg whites, apple juice concentrate, Splenda, and 1¼ cups of the skim milk. Add the milk mixture to the dry ingredients and mix well, but do not overmix. Add the remaining milk if necessary to reach the desired consistency.

2. Cook the pancakes in a nonstick skillet or on a griddle treated with nonstick spray over medium heat.

## Serves 2

1 cup whole-wheat flour
½ cup buckwheat flour
1½ teaspoons baking powder
2 egg whites
¼ cup apple juice concentrate, no sugar added
½ cup Splenda
1¼ to 1½ cups skim milk

### NUTRITIONAL ANALYSIS
(per serving):

Calories: 220
Protein: 11 g
Carbohydrate: 44 g
Fat: 1 g
Sat. Fat: 0 g
Cholesterol: 1 mg
Sodium: 200 mg
Fiber: 5 g
Exchange Approx.:
2 Breads, ½ Skim Milk, ½ Fruit

# Berry Puff Pancakes

**Serves 6**

2 large whole eggs
1 large egg white
½ cup skim milk
½ cup all-purpose flour
1 tablespoon Splenda granular
⅛ teaspoon sea salt
2 cups of fresh berries,
    such as raspberries,
    blackberries, boysenberries,
    blueberries, strawberries,
    or a combination

---

## NUTRITIONAL ANALYSIS

(per serving):

Calories: 95
Protein: 5 g
Carbohydrate: 14 g
Fat: 2 g
Sat. Fat: 1 g
Cholesterol: 71 mg
Sodium: 83 mg
Fiber: 3 g
Exchange Approx.:
1 Bread, ½ Fruit

1. Preheat oven to 450°F. Treat a 10-inch oven-proof skillet or deep pie pan with nonstick spray. Once the oven is heated, place the pan in the oven for a few minutes to get it hot.

2. Add the eggs and egg white to a medium bowl and beat until mixed. Whisk in the milk. Slowly whisk in the flour, Splenda granular, and salt.

3. Remove the preheated pan from the oven and pour the batter into it. Bake for 15 minutes. Reduce the heat to 350°F and bake for an additional 10 minutes, or until the batter is puffed and brown. Remove from the oven and slide the puffed pancake onto a serving plate. Cover the pancake with the fruit. Cut into 6 equal wedges and serve.

## Syrup Substitutes

Spreading 2 teaspoons of your favorite sugar-free jam or jelly on a waffle or pancake not only gives you a sweet topping, it can be one of your Free Exchange List choices for the day.

# Buttermilk Pancakes

1. Blend together all the ingredients, adding more water if necessary, to get the batter consistency you desire.

2. Pour a quarter of the batter into a nonstick skillet or a skillet treated with nonstick cooking spray. Cook over medium heat until bubbles appear on the top half of the pancake. Flip and continue cooking until the center of pancake is done. Repeat process with remaining batter.

## Nut Butter Batter

For a change of pace, try adding 1 Exchange amount per serving of nut butter to pancake batter and then use sugar-free jelly or jam instead of syrup.

**Serves 2**

1 cup all-purpose flour
2 tablespoons nonfat
    buttermilk powder
¼ teaspoon baking soda
½ teaspoon low-salt baking
    powder
1 cup water

---

**NUTRITIONAL ANALYSIS**
(per serving):

Calories: 143
Protein: 6 g
Carbohydrate: 26 g
Fat: 2 g
Sat. Fat: 1 g
Cholesterol: 49 mg
Sodium: 111 mg
Fiber: 1 g
Exchange Approx.:
1½ Breads

# Sweet Potato Flour Crêpes

**Yields 10 crêpes**
**Serving size: 1 crêpe**

2 eggs
¾ cup Ener-G sweet potato flour
½ teaspoon vanilla*
1 cup skim milk
1 tablespoon nonfat dry milk
Pinch of sea salt

---

### NUTRITIONAL ANALYSIS
(per serving):

Calories: 67
Protein: 3 g
Carbohydrate: 11 g
Fat: 1 g
Sat. Fat: trace
Cholesterol: 38 mg
Sodium: 42 mg
Fiber: trace
Exchange Approx.:
1 Bread/Starch

*Vanilla extract contains a trace amount of sugar. You can substitute sugar-free organic extract if you prefer.*

1. Put all the ingredients in a blender or food processor and process until the mixture is the consistency of cream.

2. To prepare the crêpes, treat an 8-inch non-stick skillet heated over medium heat with non-stick spray. Pour about 2 tablespoons of the crêpe batter into the hot pan, tilting in a circular motion until the batter spreads evenly over the pan. Cook the crêpe until the outer edges just begin to brown and loosen from the pan. Flip the crêpe to the other side and cook about 30 seconds. Using a thin spatula, lift the crêpe from the pan and place on warm plate. Continue until all the crêpes are done.

# Eggs Benedict Redux

1. Toast the bread and poach the egg.

2. Place the salmon over the top of the toasted bread. Top the salmon with the poached egg.

3. Stir the lemon juice into the yogurt and spoon that mixture over the top of the egg; serve immediately.

**Serves 1**

1 (2-ounce) slice reduced-
  calorie oat bran bread
1 egg
1 ounce Ducktrap River
  smoked salmon
2 tablespoons nonfat plain
  yogurt
1 teaspoon fresh lemon juice

**NUTRITIONAL ANALYSIS**
(per serving):

Calories: 318
Protein: 18 g
Carbohydrate: 37 g
Fat: 11 g
Sat. Fat: 3 g
Cholesterol: 195 mg
Sodium: 698 mg
Fiber: 2 g
Exchange Approx.:
1 Lean Meat, 1 Medium-
Fat Meat, 2 Breads,
1 Free Condiment

# Fruit Smoothie

## Serves 1

1 cup skim milk
2 Exchange servings of any
diced fruit
1 tablespoon honey
4 teaspoons toasted wheat
germ
6 large ice cubes

---

**NUTRITIONAL ANALYSIS**
(per serving):

The Nutritional Analy-
sis and Fruit Exchange
for this recipe will
depend on your
choice of fruit. Other-
wise, allow ½ Skim
Milk Exchange and ½
Misc. Food Exchange.
The wheat germ adds
fiber, but at less than
20 calories a serving,
it can count as 1 Free
Exchange.

---

Put all the ingredients into a blender or food
processor and process until thick and smooth!

## Batch 'Em

Make large batches of smoothies so you can
keep single servings in the freezer. Get out a
serving as you begin to get ready for your day.
This should give the smoothie time to thaw
enough for you to stir it when you're ready to
have breakfast.

# Tofu Smoothie

In a food processor or blender, process all the ingredients until smooth. Add a little chilled water for thinner smoothies if desired.

**Serves 1**

1⅓ cups frozen unsweetened strawberries
½ of a banana
½ cup (4 ounces) silken tofu

---

**NUTRITIONAL ANALYSIS**
(per serving):

Calories: 288
Protein: 20 g
Carbohydrate: 35 g
Fat: 11 g
Sat. Fat: 2 g
Cholesterol: 0 mg
Sodium: 19 mg
Fiber: 9 g
Exchange Approx.:
1 Meat Substitute,
2 Fruits

# Overnight Oatmeal

**Serves 4**

1 cup steel-cut oats
14 dried apricot halves
1 dried fig
2 tablespoons golden raisins
4 cups water
½ cup Mock Cream (see page 20)

Add all the ingredients to a slow cooker with a ceramic interior, and set to low heat. Cover and cook overnight (for 8 to 9 hours).

# Egg Clouds on Toast

1. In a copper bowl, beat the egg whites until they thicken. Add the Splenda granular, and continue to beat until stiff peaks form.

2. In a small saucepan, heat the water and apple juice over medium heat until it just begins to boil; reduce heat and allow mixture to simmer. Drop the egg whites by the tea-spoonful into the simmering water. Simmer for 3 minutes, then turn the egg white "clouds" over and simmer for an additional 3 minutes.

3. Ladle the "clouds" over the bread and serve immediately.

*TIP: Additional serving suggestions: Spread 1 teaspoon of sugar-free or all-fruit spread on the toast (½ Fruit Exchange) before you ladle on the "clouds." Or, for cinnamon French-style toast, sprinkle ¼ teaspoon cinnamon over the top of the clouds.*

**Serves 1**

2 egg whites
½ teaspoon Splenda granular
1 tablespoon frozen apple juice concentrate
1 cup water
1 slice oat bran bread, lightly toasted

**NUTRITIONAL ANALYSIS**
(per serving):

Calories: 118
Protein: 10 g
Carbohydrate: 16 g
Fat: 1 g
Sat. Fat: trace
Cholesterol: 0 mg
Sodium: 242 mg
Fiber: 2 g
Exchange Approx.:
½ Very Lean Meat,
½ Bread

# Main Courses and Casseroles

chapter four

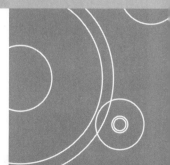

# Condensed Cream of Mushroom Soup

**Yields equivalent of 1
(10.75-ounce) can**

½ cup water
⅛ cup Ener-G potato flour
¾ cup finely chopped fresh
mushrooms
Optional ingredients:
1 teaspoon chopped onion
1 tablespoon of chopped
celery

---

**NUTRITIONAL ANALYSIS**
(per recipe):

Calories: 92
Protein: 3 g
Carbohydrate: 21 g
Fat: trace
Sat. Fat: trace
Cholesterol: 0 mg
Sodium: 13 mg
Fiber: 3 g
Exchange Approx.:
will depend on the
serving size and soup
preparation method

1. In a microwave-safe, covered container, microwave the chopped mushrooms (and the onion and celery, if using) for 2 minutes, or until tender. (About ¾ cup of chopped mushrooms will yield a half cup of steamed ones.) Reserve any resulting liquid from the steamed mushrooms, and then add enough water to equal 1 cup.

2. Place all the ingredients in a blender and process. The thickness of this soup concentrate will vary according to how much moisture remains in the mushrooms. If necessary, add 1–2 tablespoons of water to achieve a paste. Low-sodium, canned mushrooms work in this recipe, but the Nutritional Analysis assumes that fresh mushrooms are used. Adjust the sodium content accordingly.

## Potato Flour Substitute?

Instant mashed potatoes can replace potato flour; however, the amount needed will vary according to the brand of potatoes. Also, you'll need to consider other factors such as added fats and hydrogenated oils.

# Condensed Cream of Chicken Soup, Minor's Base Method

Place all the ingredients in a blender and process until well blended. As you can tell from the Nutritional Analysis of this recipe, this condensed soup made using Minor's Low-Sodium Chicken Broth Base has only half of the fat of the below recipe, and the total calories are less, too. The biggest difference is in the amount of sodium; this version has only a fifth (20 percent) of the sodium that is in the recipe using canned broth.

## Condensed Cream of Chicken Soup

For the equivalent of 1 (10.75-ounce) can of condensed chicken soup, blend 1 cup reduced fat canned chicken broth with ¼ cup Ener-G potato flour. The recipe will last, refrigerated, for 3 days. The Nutritional Analysis for the entire recipe is: Calories: 181; Protein: 8 g; Carbohydrate: 34 g; Fat: 2 g; Sat. Fat: trace g; Cholesterol: 0 mg; Sodium: 785 mg; Fiber: 2 g; PCF Ratio: 17-76-7. Exchange Approximations will depend on the serving size and soup preparation method.

**Yields equivalent of 1 (10.75-ounce) can**

1 cup water
¾ teaspoon Minor's Low-Sodium Chicken Base
¼ cup Ener-G potato flour

**NUTRITIONAL ANALYSIS**
(per recipe):

Calories: 158
Protein: 4 g
Carbohydrate: 35 g
Fat: 1 g
Sat. Fat: trace
Cholesterol: 1 mg
Sodium: 162 mg
Fiber: 2 g
Exchange Approx.: will depend on the serving size and soup preparation method

# Condensed Cream of Celery Soup

### Yields equivalent of 1 (10.75-ounce) can

½ cup water
⅛ cup Ener-G potato flour
½ cup steamed, chopped celery

---

### NUTRITIONAL ANALYSIS
(per recipe):

Calories: 85
Protein: 2 g
Carbohydrate: 20 g
Fat: trace
Sat. Fat: trace
Cholesterol: 0 mg
Sodium: 79 mg
Fiber: 2 g
Exchange Approx.: will depend on the serving size and soup preparation method

1. In a microwave-safe, covered container, microwave the chopped celery for 2 minutes, or until tender. Do not drain off any of the resulting liquid. If necessary, add enough water to bring the steamed celery and liquid to 1 cup total.

2. Place all the ingredients in a blender and process. Use immediately, or store in a covered container in the refrigerator for use within 3 days. The thickness of this concentrate will depend upon how much moisture remains in the celery; add 1–2 tablespoons of water, if necessary, to achieve a paste.

# Condensed Cream of Potato Soup

1. Place the potatoes and water in a covered, microwave-safe bowl and microwave on high for 4 to 5 minutes, until the potatoes are fork-tender.

2. Pour the potatoes and water into a blender, being careful of the steam. Remove the vent from the blender lid and process until smooth. Add the Ener-G potato flour 1 teaspoon at a time while the blender is running.

*Tip: The Nutritional Analysis for this recipe assumes you'll use the entire tablespoon of Ener-G potato flour; however, the amount needed will depend on the amount of starch in the potatoes you use. For example, new potatoes will require more Ener-G potato flour than will larger, Idaho-style potatoes.*

**Yields equivalent of 1 (10.75-ounce) can**

½ cup peeled, diced potatoes
½ cup water
1 tablespoon Ener-G potato flour

---

**NUTRITIONAL ANALYSIS**
(per recipe):

Calories: 103
Protein: 2 g
Carbohydrate: 24 g
Fat: trace
Sat. Fat: trace
Cholesterol: 0 mg
Sodium: 9 mg
Fiber: 2 g
Exchange Approx.: will depend on the serving size and soup preparation method

# Condensed Tomato Soup

## Yields equivalent of 1 (10.75-ounce) can

1 cup peeled, chopped tomato, with the juice
¼ teaspoon baking soda
Additional tomato juices (if necessary)
⅛ cup Ener-G potato flour

---

### NUTRITIONAL ANALYSIS
(per serving):

Calories: 136
Protein: 4 g
Carbohydrate: 31 g
Fat: 1 g
Sat. Fat: trace
Cholesterol: 0 mg
Sodium: 352 mg
Fiber: 4 g
Exchange Approx.: will depend on the serving size and soup preparation method

1. Place the tomato in a microwave-safe bowl and microwave on high for 2 to 3 minutes, until the tomato is cooked. Add additional tomato juices if necessary to bring the mixture back up to 1 cup.

2. Add the baking soda and vigorously stir until the bubbling stops. Pour the cooked tomato mixture into a blender; add the potato flour, 1 tablespoon at a time, processing until well blended.

*TIP: The Nutritional Analysis for this recipe assumes you use 2 tablespoons (⅛ cup) of potato flour; however, the amount needed will depend on the ratio of tomato pulp to juice. The juicier the cooked tomatoes, the more potato flour required.*

## Direct Preparation

If you'll be making the soup immediately after you prepare the condensed soup recipe, you can simply add your choice of the additional 1 cup of liquid (such as skim milk, soy milk, or water) to the blender and use that method to mix the milk and soup concentrate together. Pour the combined mixture into your pan or microwave-safe dish.

# Condensed Cheese Soup

This replacement for canned, condensed cheese soup is perfect in casserole recipes. Place the water, potato flour, and cottage cheese in a blender and process until well blended. Stir in the shredded cheese. The cheese will melt as the casserole is baked, prepared in the microwave, or cooked on the stovetop, according to recipe instructions.

## Be Aware of Your Exchanges

When using any of the suggested soup preparation methods, you'll need to add the appropriate Exchange Approximations for each serving amount (usually ¼ of the total) of whatever condensed soup you make. For example, broth-based soups like chicken and cream of mushroom or celery would be a Free Exchange. The cream of potato soup would add 1 Carbohydrate/Starch.

**Yields equivalent of 1 (10.75-ounce) can**

½ cup water
⅛ cup Ener-G potato flour
¼ cup nonfat cottage cheese
2 ounces American, Cheddar, or Colby Cheese, shredded (to yield ½ cup)

**NUTRITIONAL ANALYSIS** (per recipe):

Calories: 315
Protein: 20 g
Carbohydrate: 18 g
Fat: 18 g
Sat. Fat: 11 g
Cholesterol: 56 mg
Sodium: 384 mg
Fiber: 1 g
Exchange Approx.: will depend on the serving size and soup preparation method

# Soup Preparation Method I: Stovetop

**Serves 4**

**NUTRITIONAL ANALYSIS**
(per serving, skim milk):

Additional Calories: 21
Protein: 2 g
Carbohydrate: 3 g
Fat: trace
Sat. Fat: trace
Cholesterol: 1 mg
Sodium: 32 mg
Fiber: 0 g
Exchange Approx.:
1 Low-Fat Milk for
entire pot of soup;
divide accordingly per
serving

1. To use any of the homemade condensed soup recipes as soup, add 1 cup of skim milk (or soy milk or water) to a pan.

2. Stir using a spoon or whisk to blend. Cook over medium heat until mixture begins to simmer. Season according to taste.

# Soup Preparation
# Method II: Microwave

1. Add your choice of condensed soup and 1 cup of skim milk (or soy milk or water) to a 2-quart microwave-safe dish with a cover.

2. Stir using a spoon or whisk to blend. Microwave, covered, on high for 1 to 3 minutes, until soup is hot. Do not boil.

**Serves 4**

**NUTRITIONAL ANALYSIS**
(per serving, skim milk):

Additional Calories: 21
Protein: 2 g
Carbohydrate: 3 g
Fat: trace
Sat. Fat: trace
Cholesterol: 1 mg
Sodium: 32 mg
Fiber: 0 g
Exchange Approx.:
1 Low-Fat Milk for
entire pot of soup;
divide accordingly per
serving

# Soup Preparation III: Extra-Rich Creamed Soup

**Serves 4**

1 cup skim milk
¼ cup nonfat milk powder
4 teaspoons unsalted butter

---

**NUTRITIONAL ANALYSIS**
(per serving):

Additional Calories: 71
Protein: 4 g
Carbohydrate: 5 g
Fat: 4 g
Sat. Fat: 2 g
Cholesterol: 12 mg
Sodium: 56 mg
Fiber: 0 g
Exchange Approx.:
1 Milk, 1 Fat for entire
pot of soup; divide
accordingly per
serving

1. In a saucepan, whisk together the skim milk, milk powder, and your choice of 1 recipe of condensed soup; warm on medium-low heat.

2. Add the butter 1 teaspoon at a time, allowing each teaspoon to melt and stirring to fully incorporate it into the mixture before adding more.

3. Heat to serving temperature, stirring constantly; do not allow the mixture to boil. The butter in this extra-rich version will affect its fat content, so check with your dietitian to determine whether it's okay to make your soup this way.

## Condensed Soup Casserole Guidelines

The casseroles in this section use the condensed soup recipes in this chapter. If you substitute canned, condensed soup, be sure to adjust the Exchange Approximations when necessary.

# Traditional Stovetop Tuna-Noodle Casserole

1. Cook the egg noodles according to package directions. Drain and return to pan.

2. Add all the ingredients to the pan; stir to blend. Cook over medium heat, stirring occasionally, until the cheese is melted. (1⅓ cups of dried egg noodles will yield 2 cups of cooked egg noodles. The Nutritional Analysis for this recipe assumes that the egg noodles were cooked without salt.)

## Extra-Rich Stovetop Tuna-Noodle Casserole

Add 1 medium egg (beaten) and 1 tablespoon mayonnaise to give this casserole the taste of rich, homemade egg noodles, while—at 21 percent of total calories—still maintaining a good fat ratio. It's still less than 300 calories per serving, too! The per-serving Nutritional Analysis is: Calories: 275; Protein: 21 g; Carbohydrate: 34 g; Fat: 7 g; Sat. Fat: 2 g; Cholesterol: 94 mg; Sodium: 281 mg; Fiber: 4 g; PCF Ratio: 30-48-21. Exchange Approximations: 1½ Bread, 1 Vegetable, 1 Meat, 1 Medium Meat Fat.

**Serves 4**

2 cups cooked egg noodles
1 recipe Condensed Cream of Mushroom Soup (see page 60)
1 teaspoon steamed, chopped onion
1 tablespoon steamed, chopped celery
½ cup skim milk
1 ounce American, Cheddar, or Colby cheese, shredded (to yield ¼ cup)
1 cup frozen mixed peas and carrots
1 cup steamed, sliced fresh mushrooms
1 can water-packed tuna, drained

**NUTRITIONAL ANALYSIS**
(per serving):

Calories: 245
Protein: 20 g
Carbohydrate: 33 g
Fat: 4 g
Sat. Fat: 2 g
Cholesterol: 46 mg
Sodium: 241 mg
Fiber: 4 g
Exchange Approx.:
1½ Breads, 1 Vegetable, 1 Medium Fat Meat

# Chicken and Mushroom Rice Casserole

## Serves 8

1 recipe Condensed Cream
   of Chicken Soup (see page
   61)
1 cup diced chicken breast
1 large onion, chopped
½ cup chopped celery
1 cup uncooked rice (not
   instant rice)
Freshly ground black pepper
   to taste (optional)
2 cups boiling water
2½ cups chopped broccoli
   flowerets
1 cup sliced fresh mushrooms

### NUTRITIONAL ANALYSIS
(per serving):

Calories: 165
Protein: 9 g
Carbohydrate: 30 g
Fat: 1 g
Sat. Fat: trace
Cholesterol: 15 mg
Sodium: 41 mg
Fiber: 3 g
Exchange Approx.:
1 Very Lean Meat,
1 Bread/Starch,
1 Vegetable

1. Preheat oven to 350°F. In a 4-quart casserole dish (large enough to prevent boil-overs in the oven) that's been treated with nonstick spray, combine the condensed soup, chicken breast, onion, celery, rice, and seasonings; mix well. Pour the boiling water over the top of the mixture, and bake, covered, for 30 minutes.

2. Stir the casserole, adding the broccoli and mushrooms, replace the cover, and return to the oven to bake for an additional 20 to 30 minutes, or until the celery is tender and the rice has absorbed all the liquid.

## Base Basics

An easy way to add rich flavor to the condensed soup or casserole recipes without adding extra calories is to use ⅛ to ¼ teaspoon of other Minor's bases, like Roasted Mirepoix, Onion, or Garlic.

# Italian Ground Turkey Casserole

1. Place the ground turkey in a large, covered skillet over medium-low heat and allow it to steam, being careful not to brown the meat. Drain off the grease and use paper towels to blot the meat to absorb any excess fat from the turkey. Add the onion, mushrooms, minced garlic, and herbs, and toss lightly. Return the cover to the skillet and steam the vegetables until they are tender, about 3 minutes. Set aside.

2. Put the shredded cabbage in a large, covered microwave-safe dish and steam until the cabbage is crisp-tender, about 5 minutes. (If your microwave doesn't have a carousel, turn the dish about halfway through the cooking time.) Drain the cabbage in a colander, being careful not to burn yourself from the steam. Press out any excess moisture.

3. Mix the cottage cheese, potato flour, and half of the Parmesan and mozzarella cheeses together. Add the condensed tomato soup, tomato paste, and canned tomatoes to the meat mixture and stir well.

4. Preheat oven to 350°F. Coat a deep rectangular baking dish or roasting pan with non-stick spray. Spoon a third of the meat mixture into the bottom of the pan. Top with half of the cooked cabbage. Add another third of the meat mixture. Top that with the cottage cheese mixture, and the rest of the cabbage. Add the remaining meat mixture and sprinkle the top of the casserole with the remaining Parmesan and mozzarella cheeses.

5. Bake for 45 minutes, or until the casserole is heated through and the cheeses on top are melted and bubbling.

**Serves 8**

1 pound ground turkey or turkey sausage
1 large onion, chopped
2 cups sliced fresh mushrooms
1 teaspoon minced garlic
1 teaspoon dried basil
¼ teaspoon dried oregano
½ teaspoon dried parsley
6 cups shredded cabbage
2 cups nonfat cottage cheese
⅛ cup Ener-G potato flour
4 ounces Parmesan cheese, grated (to yield 1 cup)
4 ounces part-skim mozzarella cheese, grated (to yield 1 cup)
1 recipe Condensed Tomato Soup (see page 64)
1 (6-ounce) can salt-free tomato paste
1 (16-ounce) can salt-free diced tomatoes

**NUTRITIONAL ANALYSIS**
(per serving):

Calories: 298
Protein: 29 g
Carbohydrate: 23 g
Fat: 12 g
Sat. Fat: 6 g
Cholesterol: 67 mg
Sodium: 462 mg
Fiber: 5 g
Exchange Approx.:
3 Medium Fat Meats,
2 Vegetables, ¼ Bread

# Aloha Ham Microwave Casserole

**Serves 4**

1⅓ cups cooked rice
1 medium onion, chopped
1 recipe Condensed Cream of Celery Soup (see page 62)
1 (8-ounce) can pineapple chunks in juice
¼ cup water
1 teaspoon honey
½ pound (8 ounces) sliced lean baked or boiled ham
Sliced green onions, for garnish (optional)

---

**NUTRITIONAL ANALYSIS**

(per serving):

Calories: 214
Protein: 14 g
Carbohydrate: 32 g
Fat: 3 g
Sat. Fat: 1 g
Cholesterol: 27 mg
Sodium: 834 mg
Fiber: 1 g
Exchange Approx.:
1 Lean Meat, 1 Bread/
Starch, 1 Fruit

1. Cook the rice according to package directions. Put the rice in a casserole dish and set aside. Place the chopped onion in a microwave-safe, covered bowl and microwave on high until tender, about 1 minute. Add the soup, pineapple with juice, water, and honey to the onion. Heat, covered, on high until the mixture begins to boil, about 1 minute. Stir mixture until the honey is dissolved.

2. Pour half of the soup mixture over the rice. Arrange the ham slices on top of the rice and pour the remaining soup mixture over it. Cover loosely with plastic wrap or a paper towel (to prevent splatters in the microwave) and heat on high until the rice is reheated and ham is warm, about 1 minute. (If you are on a sodium-restricted diet, consider substituting chicken or turkey breast for the ham.)

# Shrimp Microwave Casserole

1. Cook the egg noodles according to package directions and keep warm. Place the green onion and green pepper in a covered, microwave-safe dish and microwave on high for 1 minute. Add the mushroom slices and microwave for another minute, or until all the vegetables are tender.

2. Add the soup, Worcestershire sauce, Tabasco (if using), pimiento, ripe olives, and milk, and stir well. Microwave covered for 1 to 2 minutes until the mixture is hot and bubbly.

3. Add the cooked shrimp and noodles and stir to mix; microwave for another 30 seconds to 1 minute, or until the mixture is hot.

**Serves 4**

1⅓ uncooked egg noodles (to yield 4½ (½-cup) servings)
1 cup chopped green onion
1 cup chopped green pepper
1 cup sliced mushrooms
1 recipe Condensed Cream of Celery Soup (see page 62)
1 teaspoon Worcestershire sauce (see recipe for Homemade Worcestershire on page 17)
4 drops Tabasco (optional)
¼ cup diced canned pimientos
½ cup pitted, chopped ripe olives
½ cup skim milk
½ pound (8 ounces) cooked, deveined, shelled shrimp

---

**NUTRITIONAL ANALYSIS**
(per serving):

Calories: 196
Protein: 17 g
Carbohydrate: 27 g
Fat: 2 g
Sat. Fat: trace
Cholesterol: 131 mg
Sodium: 290 mg
Fiber: 2 g
Exchange Approx.:
1 Starch, 1 Vegetable,
1 Medium-Fat Meat

# Single-Serving Beef (Almost) Stroganoff

**Serves 1**

1 tablespoon steamed or low-fat sautéed diced celery
1 teaspoon diced onion, steamed or low-fat sautéed
½ cup sliced mushrooms, steamed or low-fat sautéed
1 cup shredded, unseasoned cabbage, steamed
½ cup cooked egg noodles
¼ cup nonfat cottage cheese
1 teaspoon finely grated Parmesan cheese
½ teaspoon Ener-G potato flour
1 clove roasted garlic (for roasting instructions, see Dry-Roasted Garlic on page 31)
1 tablespoon nonfat yogurt or nonfat sour cream
1 ounce lean roast beef, pulled or cubed
⅛ teaspoon nutmeg

1. Toss the celery, onion, mushrooms, cabbage, and noodles together in a microwave-safe, covered serving dish.

2. Put the cheeses, roasted garlic, potato flour, and yogurt (or sour cream) in a blender and process until smooth. Lightly mix the cheese sauce with the vegetables, then top the vegetables with the roast beef and sprinkle the nutmeg over the top of the dish. Microwave, covered, on high for 1 to 2 minutes, or until heated through.

**NUTRITIONAL ANALYSIS**
(per serving):

Calories: 286
Protein: 24 g
Carbohydrate: 37 g
Fat: 6 g
Sat. Fat: 2 g
Cholesterol: 53 mg
Sodium: 105 mg
Fiber: 6 g
Exchange Approx.:
1 Very Lean Meat,
1 Lean Meat, 1 Free,
1 Vegetable, 1 Starch

# Single-Serving Smoked Turkey Casserole

In a covered, microwave-safe bowl, combine all the ingredients and microwave on high for 1 to 2 minutes, or until heated through.

**Serves 1**

1 tablespoon steamed or low-fat sautéed diced celery
1 teaspoon diced onion, steamed or low-fat sautéed
1 tablespoon diced green pepper, steamed or low-fat sautéed
½ cup sliced mushrooms, steamed or low-fat sautéed
1 ounce smoked turkey, diced or thinly sliced
¼ cup nonfat cottage cheese
1 teaspoon finely grated Parmesan cheese
½ teaspoon Ener-G potato flour
½ cup cooked egg noodles

**NUTRITIONAL ANALYSIS**
(per serving):

Calories: 221
Protein: 18 g
Carbohydrate: 27 g
Fat: 5 g
Sat. Fat: 2 g
Cholesterol: 46 mg
Sodium: 363 mg
Fiber: 3 g
Exchange Approx.:
2 Lean Meats,
1 Starch, 1 Vegetable

# Single-Serving Salmon Scramble

**Serves 1**

1 cup chopped broccoli (fresh
  or frozen)
1 medium egg
½ teaspoon Hellmann's or
  Best Foods tartar sauce
1½ teaspoons yellow cornmeal
2 Keebler low-salt soda
  crackers, crumbled
2 ounces canned salmon,
  drained

1. In a microwave-safe, covered bowl, steam the broccoli for 5 minutes, or until tender. Drain any moisture from the broccoli; add it to a non-stick skillet treated with nonstick spray, and dry-sauté it to remove any excess moisture.

2. In another bowl, beat the egg and mix in the tartar sauce, cornmeal, cracker crumbs, and salmon. Pour the salmon mixture over the broccoli and toss to mix. Cook over medium-low heat until the egg is done, stirring the mixture occasionally with a spatula.

**NUTRITIONAL ANALYSIS**
(per serving):

Calories: 222
Protein: 22 g
Carbohydrate: 12 g
Fat: 10 g
Sat. Fat: 3 g
Cholesterol: 0 mg
Sodium: 421 mg
Fiber: 5 g
Exchange Approx.:
2 Lean Meats,
1 Medium-Fat Meat,
½ Bread, 1 Vegetable

# Single-Serving Unstuffed Cabbage and Green Peppers

1. In a microwave-safe, covered dish, microwave the ground round, oregano, garlic, parsley, ginger, mustard, celery, onion, and green pepper for 2 minutes. Stir the mixture, being careful not to burn yourself on the steam. Microwave on high for another 2 to 3 minutes, or until the meat is no longer pink. Drain any fat residue or dab the beef mixture with a paper towel.

2. Heat the steamed cabbage in the microwave on high for 30 seconds to 1 minute to warm it to serving temperature. Toss the chopped, raw tomato with the ground round mixture and spoon it over the warmed cabbage. Sprinkle the dried basil over the top of the dish and serve. (If you serve this dish over ½ cup cooked rice instead of cabbage, add 1 Starch Exchange.)

**Serves 1**

3 ounces uncooked Laura's Lean Beef ground round
⅛ teaspoon dried oregano
¼ teaspoon minced, dried garlic (or ½ clove minced fresh garlic)
¼ teaspoon dried parsley
Dash of dried ginger
Dash of dried mustard
2 tablespoons chopped celery
2 tablespoons chopped onion
1 cup chopped green pepper
½ cup steamed cabbage, shredded or rough chopped
1 medium peeled, chopped tomato
¼ teaspoon dried basil

**NUTRITIONAL ANALYSIS**
(per serving):

Calories: 207
Protein: 16 g
Carbohydrate: 14 g
Fat: 10 g
Sat. Fat: 4 g
Cholesterol: 46 mg
Sodium: 55 mg
Fiber: 4 g
Exchange Approx.:
2 Lean Meats, 2 Vegetables, 1 Free

# Poultry and Meats

## chapter five

# Chicken Broth: Easy Slow-Cooker Method

**Yield about 4 cups**
**Serving size: ½ cup**

1 small onion, chopped
2 carrots, peeled and chopped
2 celery stalks and leaves,
    chopped
1 bay leaf
4 sprigs parsley
6 black peppercorns
¼ cup dry white wine
2 pounds chicken pieces, skin
    removed
4½ cups water

---

**NUTRITIONAL ANALYSIS**
(per serving):

Calories: 67

Protein: 9 g

Carbohydrate: 0 g

Fat: 3 g

Sat. Fat: 1 g

Cholesterol: 24 mg

Sodium: 22 mg

Fiber: 0 g

Exchange Approx.:
½ Very Lean Meat,
½ Lean Meat

1. Add all ingredients except the water to the slow cooker. The chicken pieces and vegetables should be loosely layered and fill no more than ¾ of the slow cooker. Add enough water to just cover the ingredients, and cover the slow cooker. Use the high setting until the mixture almost reaches a boil, then reduce heat to low. Allow to simmer overnight or up to 16 hours, checking occasionally and adding more water, if necessary.

2. Remove the chicken pieces and drain on paper towels to absorb any fat. Allow to cool, then remove the meat from the bones. Strain the vegetables from the broth and discard. (You don't want to eat vegetables cooked directly with the chicken because they will have absorbed too much of the residue fat.) Put the broth in a covered container and refrigerate for several hours or overnight, allowing the fat to congeal on top of the broth. Remove the hardened fat and discard.

3. To separate the broth into small amounts for use when you steam vegetables or potatoes, fill up an ice cube tray with stock. Let freeze, then remove the cubes from the tray and store in a labeled freezer bag. (Note the size of the ice cubes. Common ice cube trays allow for ⅛ cup or 2 tablespoons of liquid per section.)

*TIP: The broth will be richer than what most recipes call for, so unless you need "reduced" broth, thin the broth with water as needed.*

## Know Your Terms

Reducing broth is the act of boiling it to decrease the amount of water, so you're left with a richer broth.

# Oven-Fried Chicken Thighs

1. Preheat oven to 350°F. Rinse and dry the chicken thighs. Put the white flour on a plate. In a small, shallow bowl, whip the egg white together with the sea salt; add the olive oil, if using, and mix well. Put the rice flour and corn-meal on another plate and mix them together. Place a rack on a baking sheet and spray both with nonstick cooking spray.

2. Roll each chicken thigh in the white flour, dip it into the egg mixture, and then roll it in the rice flour mixture. Place the chicken thighs on the rack so that they aren't touching. Bake for 35 to 45 minutes, until the meat juices run clear.

*TIP: Boneless, skinless chicken breast strips will work, although the meat tends to be drier. Allow 1 Very Lean Meat Exchange List choice for each 1-ounce serving.*

**Serves 4**

4 chicken thighs, skin removed
1 tablespoon unbleached, white all-purpose flour
1 large egg white
½ teaspoon sea salt
1 tablespoon rice flour
½ teaspoon olive oil (optional; see the "with olive oil" Comparison Analysis)
1 tablespoon cornmeal

**COMPARISON ANALYSIS (WITH OLIVE OIL)**

Calories: 78.53
Protein: 9.46 g
Carbohydrate: 4.65 g
Fat: 2.27 g
Sat. Fat: 0.50 g
Cholesterol: 34.03 mg
Sodium: 331.03 mg
Fiber: 0.06 g
Exchange Approx.:
2 Lean Meats

# Another Healthy "Fried" Chicken

**Serves 4**

10 ounces raw boneless,
    skinless chicken breasts
    (fat trimmed off)
½ cup nonfat plain yogurt
½ cup bread crumbs
1 teaspoon garlic powder
1 teaspoon paprika
¼ teaspoon dried thyme

## NUTRITIONAL ANALYSIS
(per serving):

Calories: 118
Protein: 19 g
Carbohydrate: 5 g
Fat: 2 g
Sat. Fat: 1 g
Cholesterol: 44 mg
Sodium: 91 mg
Fiber: trace
Exchange Approx.:
2 Very Lean Meats,
½ Starch

1. Preheat oven to 350°F and prepare a baking pan with nonstick cooking spray. Cut the chicken breast into 4 equal pieces and marinate it in the yogurt for several minutes.

2. Mix together the bread crumbs, garlic, paprika, and thyme; dredge the chicken in the crumb mixture, and arrange on prepared pan. Bake for 20 minutes. To give the chicken a deep golden color, place the pan under the broiler for the last 5 minutes of cooking. Watch closely to ensure the chicken "crust" doesn't burn.

## Chicken Fat Facts

When faced with the decision of whether to have chicken with or without the skin, consider that ½ pound of skinless chicken breast has 9 grams of fat; ½ pound with the skin on has 38 grams!

# Buttermilk Ranch
# Chicken Salad

1. In a blender or food processor, combine the mayonnaise, yogurt, cottage cheese, vinegar, honey, mustard, buttermilk, parsley, garlic, and cheese; if you're using them, add the salt and pepper at this time, too. Process until smooth. Pour this dressing over the chicken, cucumber, celery, and carrots. Chill for at least 2 hours.

2. To serve, arrange 1 cup of the salad greens on each of 4 serving plates. Top each salad with an equal amount of the chicken salad. Garnish with the red onion slices and fresh parsley, if desired.

## Get More Mileage from Your Meals

Leftover Chicken Salad makes great sandwiches. Put it and lots of lettuce between two slices of bread for a quick lunch. The lettuce helps keep the bread from getting soggy if you're preparing the sandwich "to go."

**Serves 4**

1 tablespoon Hellmann's or Best Foods Real Mayonnaise
3 tablespoons nonfat plain yogurt
½ cup nonfat cottage cheese
½ teaspoon cider vinegar
1 teaspoon honey
1 teaspoon Dijon mustard
½ cup buttermilk
2 tablespoons dried parsley
1 clove garlic, minced
2 tablespoons grated Parmesan cheese
¼ teaspoon sea salt (optional)
¼ teaspoon freshly ground pepper (optional)
1 cup chopped, cooked chicken breast
½ cup sliced cucumber
½ cup chopped celery
½ cup sliced carrots
4 cups salad greens
½ cup red onion slices
Fresh parsley for garnish

**NUTRITIONAL ANALYSIS**
(per serving):

Calories: 166
Protein: 19 g
Carbohydrate: 11 g
Fat: 5 g
Sat. Fat: 2 g
Cholesterol: 34 mg
Sodium: 412 mg
Fiber: 2 g
Exchange Approx.: 2 Very Lean Meats, ½ Vegetable, 1 Free Vegetable, ½ Skim Milk

# Molded Chicken Salad

**Serves 12**

½ cup nonfat plain yogurt
2 envelopes unflavored gelatin
¼ cup boiling water
1 teaspoon cider vinegar
1 teaspoon Dijon mustard
1 teaspoon honey
1 tablespoon Hellmann's
  or Best Foods Real
  Mayonnaise
½ cup nonfat cottage cheese
4 ounces cream cheese
1 teaspoon celery seed
½ cup chopped dill pickle
¼ cup chopped green onion
  (scallions)
1 recipe Condensed Cream
  of Chicken Soup (see page
  61)
1½ pounds (24 ounces)
  cooked, chopped chicken

1. Put the yogurt in a blender or food processor and sprinkle the gelatin on top; let stand for 2 minutes to soften the gelatin.

2. Add the boiling water and process until the gelatin is dissolved. Add the remaining ingredients except for the chicken and process until smooth. Fold in the chopped chicken, and taste for seasonings. Herbs like chopped chives, a little more cider vinegar, or ground black pepper won't affect Exchange Approximations.

3. Pour into a mold or terrine treated with nonstick spray and chill until firm.

---

**NUTRITIONAL ANALYSIS**

(per serving):

Calories: 174
Protein: 22 g
Carbohydrate: 5 g
Fat: 7 g
Sat. Fat: 3 g
Cholesterol: 60 mg
Sodium: 267 mg
Fiber: trace
Exchange Approx.:
1 Very Lean Meat,
1 Lean Meat, 1½ Fats,
½ Skim Milk

# Chicken and Broccoli Casserole

1. Preheat oven to 350°F. Treat an 11" × 7" casserole dish with nonstick spray. Steam the broccoli until tender; drain.

2. Spread out the chicken on the bottom of the dish and cover it with the broccoli. Combine the milk, mayonnaise, soup, curry powder, and lemon juice; pour over broccoli. Mix together the cheese, bread crumbs, butter, and oil; sprinkle over the top of the casserole. Bake for 30 minutes.

**Serves 4**

2 cups broccoli
½ pound (8 ounces) cooked, chopped chicken
½ cup skim milk
⅛ cup (2 tablespoons) Hellmann's or Best Foods Real Mayonnaise
¼ teaspoon curry powder
1 recipe Condensed Cream of Chicken Soup (see page 61)
1 tablespoon lemon juice
½ cup (2 ounces) grated Cheddar cheese
½ cup bread crumbs
1 teaspoon melted butter
1 teaspoon olive oil

**NUTRITIONAL ANALYSIS**
(per serving):

Calories: 328
Protein: 26 g
Carbohydrate: 20 g
Fat: 17 g
Sat. Fat: 6 g
Cholesterol: 67 mg
Sodium: 254 mg
Fiber: 3 g
Exchange Approx.:
1 Very Lean Meat,
1 Lean Meat, ½ High-Fat Meat, 1 Fat, 1 Vegetable, 1 Skim Milk,
½ Starch

# Chicken à la King

**Serves 4**

1 recipe Condensed Cream
   of Chicken Soup (see page
   61)
¼ cup skim milk
½ teaspoon Worcestershire
   sauce (see recipe for
   Homemade on page 17)
1 tablespoon Hellmann's
   or Best Foods Real
   Mayonnaise
¼ teaspoon ground black
   pepper
2 cups frozen mix of peas and
   pearl onions, thawed
1 cup frozen sliced carrots,
   thawed
1 cup sliced mushrooms,
   steamed
½ pound (8 ounces) cooked,
   chopped chicken
4 slices whole-wheat bread,
   toasted

---

**NUTRITIONAL ANALYSIS**

(per serving):

Calories: 335
Protein: 25 g
Carbohydrate: 38 g
Fat: 10 g
Sat. Fat: 2 g
Cholesterol: 49 mg
Sodium: 299 mg
Fiber: 7 g
Exchange Approx.:
2 Lean Meats, 1 Vege-
table, 1 Starch, 1 Skim
Milk

1. Combine the soup, milk, Worcestershire,
mayonnaise, and pepper in a saucepan and
bring to a boil.

2. Reduce heat and add the peas and pearl
onions, carrots, mushrooms, and chicken.
Simmer until the vegetables and chicken are
heated through. Serve over toast.

# Chicken and Green Bean Stovetop Casserole

1. Combine the soup, milk, Worcestershire, mayonnaise, onion and garlic powder, and pepper in a saucepan and bring to a boil.

2. Reduce heat and add the water chestnuts, green beans, mushrooms, and chicken. Simmer until vegetables and chicken are heated through. Serve over rice.

## Veggie Filler

Steamed mushrooms are a low-calorie way to add flavor to a dish and "stretch" the meat. If you don't like mushrooms, you can substitute an equal amount of other low-calorie steamed vegetables like red and green peppers and not significantly affect the total calories in the recipe.

**Serves 4**

- 1 recipe Condensed Cream of Chicken Soup (see page 61)
- ¼ cup skim milk
- 2 teaspoons Worcestershire sauce (see recipe for Homemade on page 17)
- 1 teaspoon Hellmann's or Best Foods Real Mayonnaise
- ½ teaspoon onion powder
- ¼ teaspoon garlic powder
- ¼ teaspoon ground black pepper
- 1 (4-ounce) can sliced water chestnuts, drained
- 2½ cups frozen green beans, thawed
- 1 cup sliced mushrooms, steamed
- ½ pound (8 ounces) cooked, chopped chicken
- 1⅓ cups cooked brown, long-grain rice

**NUTRITIONAL ANALYSIS**
(per serving):

Calories: 305
Protein: 23 g
Carbohydrate: 36 g
Fat: 8 g
Sat. Fat: 2 g
Cholesterol: 48 mg
Sodium: 101 mg
Fiber: 6 g
Exchange Approx.:
1 Very Lean Meat,
1 Lean Meat, 1 Vegetable, 1 Starch, 1 Skim Milk

# Chicken Pasta with Herb Sauce

## Serves 4

1 recipe Condensed Cream of Chicken Soup (see page 61)
¼ cup skim milk
½ teaspoon Worcestershire sauce (see recipe for Homemade on page 17)
1 teaspoon Hellmann's or Best Foods Real Mayonnaise
¼ cup grated Parmesan cheese
¼ teaspoon chili powder
½ teaspoon garlic powder
¼ teaspoon dried rosemary
¼ teaspoon dried thyme
¼ teaspoon dried marjoram
1 cup sliced mushrooms, steamed
½ pound (8 ounces) cooked, chopped chicken
4 cups cooked pasta
Freshly ground black pepper (optional)

1. Combine the soup, milk, Worcestershire, mayonnaise, and cheese in a saucepan and bring to a boil.

2. Reduce heat and add the chili powder, garlic powder, rosemary, thyme, and marjoram; stir well.

3. Add the mushrooms and chicken and simmer until heated through. Serve over pasta, and top with freshly ground pepper, if desired.

### NUTRITIONAL ANALYSIS
(per serving):

Calories: 393
Protein: 26 g
Carbohydrate: 52 g
Fat: 8 g
Sat. Fat: 2 g
Cholesterol: 48 mg
Sodium: 71 mg
Fiber: 4 g
Exchange Approx.:
2 Lean Meats,
3 Starches, ½ Skim
Milk

# Chicken Thighs Cacciatore

1. Heat a deep, nonstick skillet over medium-high heat and add the 2 teaspoons of olive oil. Add the onion and sauté until transparent. Add the garlic and chicken thighs; sauté for 3 minutes on each side, or until lightly browned.

2. Remove the thighs from the pan and add the wine, the tomatoes and their juices, parsley, oregano, pepper, and Splenda granular. Stir well, and bring to a boil. Add the chicken back to the pan and sprinkle the Parmesan cheese over the top of the chicken and sauce. Cover, reduce heat, and simmer for 10 minutes. Uncover and simmer 10 more minutes.

3. To serve, put 1 cup of cooked pasta on each of 4 plates. Top each pasta serving with a chicken thigh and then divide the sauce between the dishes. Drizzle ½ teaspoon of extra-virgin olive oil over the top of each dish, and serve.

**Serves 4**

2 teaspoons olive oil
½ cup chopped onion
2 cloves garlic, minced
4 chicken thighs, skin removed
½ cup dry red wine
1 (14½ ounce) can unsalted diced tomatoes, undrained
1 teaspoon dried parsley
½ teaspoon dried oregano
¼ teaspoon pepper
⅛ teaspoon Splenda granular
¼ cup grated Parmesan cheese
4 cups cooked spaghetti
2 teaspoons extra-virgin olive oil

**NUTRITIONAL ANALYSIS**
(per serving):

Calories: 377
Protein: 18 g
Carbohydrate: 48 g
Fat: 11 g
Sat. Fat: 3 g
Cholesterol: 32 mg
Sodium: 150 mg
Fiber: 4 g
Exchange Approx.:
1½ Lean Meats,
2½ Starches, 1 Fat,
1 Vegetable

# Thanksgiving Feast: Turkey Casserole in a Pumpkin

**Serves 4**

4 small pumpkins
1 recipe Condensed Cream of Chicken Soup (see page 61)
1 cup skim milk
1 cup low-fat, reduced-sodium chicken broth
1 tablespoon, plus 1 teaspoon butter
½ cup steamed, diced celery
1 cup steamed, diced onion
1 cup steamed, sliced mushrooms slices
1 tablespoon cognac (optional)
Parsley, thyme, and sage to taste (optional)
1⅓ cups cubed red potatoes, steamed
½ pound (8 ounces) steamed, chopped oysters
¼ pound (4 ounces) shredded, cooked turkey
8 slices day-old bread, torn into cubes
2 eggs, beaten

## NUTRITIONAL ANALYSIS

(per serving):

Calories: 485
Protein: 30 g
Carbohydrate: 64 g
Fat: 13 g
Sat. Fat: 5 g
Cholesterol: 186 mg
Sodium: 278 mg
Fiber: 9 g
Exchange Approx.:
2 Lean Meats,
1 Medium-Fat Meat,
1 Fat, 1 Vegetable, 2
Starches, 1 Skim Milk

1. Preheat oven to 375°F. Clean the pumpkins, cut off tops, and scrape out the seeds. Put on baking sheet and cover with foil or parchment paper. Bake for 30 minutes, or until the inside flesh is somewhat tender but the pumpkins still retain their shapes.

2. While the pumpkins bake, prepare the dressing-style casserole by combining the soup, milk, broth, and butter in a saucepan; stir well to mix and bring to a boil over medium heat. Lower the heat and add the celery, onion, mushrooms, and the cognac and seasonings, if using. Simmer for 3 minutes. Remove from heat and allow to cool slightly.

3. In a large bowl, add the potatoes, oysters, turkey, and bread cubes, and toss to mix.

4. Gradually add the eggs to the soup mixture, whisking the mixture constantly; pour the mixture over the potatoes, meat, and bread cubes. Mix well to coat the bread evenly. Divide the resulting mixture into the four pumpkins. Reduce oven temperature to 350°F, and bake for 30 to 40 minutes, or until the casserole is firm. (The Analysis for this recipe assumes you'll use pumpkins that will yield ¾ cup of cooked pumpkin each.)

# Honey and Cider Glaze for Baked Chicken

1. Preheat oven to 375°F. Combine all the ingredients in a microwave safe bowl. Microwave on high for 30 seconds. Stir until the honey is dissolved.

2. To use the glaze, arrange 4 boneless chicken pieces with the skin removed on a rack placed in a roasting pan or broiling pan. Brush or spoon 1 teaspoon of glaze over the top of each piece. Baste halfway through the cooking time, and again, 5 minutes before the chicken is done. Allow the chicken to set for 5 minutes before serving.

## Spice Tea Chicken Marinade

Steep 4 Orange or Lemon Spice tea bags in 2 cups boiling water for 4 minutes. Dissolve 1 teaspoon honey into the tea, pour it over 4 chicken pieces, and marinate for 30 minutes. Occasionally turn and baste any exposed portions of chicken. Pour the tea into the roasting pan to provide moisture—discard it after cooking. Nutritional Analysis for 1 (of 4) serving: Calories: 8; Protein: trace g; Carbohydrate: 2 g; Fat: 0 g; Sat. Fat: trace g; Cholesterol: 0 mg; Sodium: 2 mg; Fiber: 0 g; PCF Ratio: 0-100-0. Exchange Approximations: ½ Free Condiment

**Serves 4**

3 tablespoons cider or apple juice
½ teaspoon honey
1 teaspoon lemon juice
1 teaspoon Bragg's Liquid Aminos
½ teaspoon lemon zest

**NUTRITIONAL ANALYSIS**
(per serving, glaze only):

Calories: 10
Protein: trace
Carbohydrate: 2 g
Fat: trace
Sat. Fat: 0 g
Cholesterol: 0 mg
Sodium: 55 mg
Fiber: trace
Exchange Approx.:
1 Free Condiment

# Beef Broth: Easy Slow-Cooker Method

**Yields about 3 cups broth**
**Serving size: ½ cup**

1 pound lean round steak
1 onion, chopped
2 carrots, peeled and chopped
2 celery stalks and leaves,
    chopped
1 bay leaf
4 sprigs parsley
6 black peppercorns
¼ cup dry white wine
4½ cups water

---

**NUTRITIONAL ANALYSIS**
(per serving):

Calories: 58
Protein: 9 g
Carbohydrate: 0 g
Fat: 2 g
Sat. Fat: 1 g
Cholesterol: 27 mg
Sodium: 14 mg
Fiber: 0 g
Exchange Approx.:
1 Lean Meat

1. Cut the beef into several pieces and add it to the slow cooker with all of the other ingredients. Use the high setting until the mixture reaches a boil, then reduce the heat to low. Allow to simmer, covered, overnight, or up to 16 hours.

2. Remove beef and drain on paper towels to absorb any fat. Strain the broth, discarding the meat and vegetables. (You don't want to eat vegetables cooked directly with the beef because they will have absorbed too much of the residue fat.) Put the broth in a covered container and refrigerate for several hours or overnight; this allows time for the fat to congeal on top of the broth. Remove the hardened fat and discard. (When you remove the fat from the broth, the Exchange Approximation for it will be a Free Exchange.)

## Trade Secrets

Some chefs swear that a hearty beef broth requires oven-roasted bones. Place bones on a roasting tray and bake them in a 425°F oven for 30 to 60 minutes. Blot the fat from the bones before adding them to the rest of the broth ingredients. You may need to reduce the amount of water in your slow cooker, which will produce a more concentrated broth.

# Stovetop Grilled Beef Loin

1. Remove the loin from the refrigerator 30 minutes before you plan to prepare it to allow it to come to room temperature. Pat the meat dry with paper towels.

2. Mix together all the dry ingredients. Combine honey with olive oil. Rub ¼ teaspoon of the olive oil on each side of the fillet. Divide the seasoning mixture and rub it into each oiled side.

3. Heat a grill pan on high for 1 or 2 minutes until the pan is sizzling hot. Place the beef fillet in the pan, reduce the heat to medium-high, and cook for 3 minutes. Use tongs to turn the fillet. (Be careful not to pierce the meat.) Cook for another 2 minutes for medium or 3 for well done.

4. Remove from heat and let the meat "rest" in the pan for at least 5 minutes, allowing the juices to redistribute throughout the meat and complete the cooking process—which makes for a juicier fillet.

## Weights and Measures: Before and After

Exchanges are based on cooking weight of meats; however, in the case of lean pork loin trimmed of all fat, very little weight is lost during the cooking process. Therefore, the amounts given for raw pork loin in the recipes equal the cooked weights. If you find your cooking method causes more variation in weight, adjust accordingly.

**Yields 1 (5-ounce) loin**
**Serving size: 1 ounce**

1 Laura's Lean Beef tenderloin
   fillet, no more than 1 inch
   thick
½ teaspoon paprika
1½ teaspoons garlic powder
⅛ teaspoon cracked black
   pepper
¼ teaspoon onion powder
Pinch to ⅛ teaspoon cayenne
   pepper (according to taste)
⅛ teaspoon dried oregano
⅛ teaspoon dried thyme
½ teaspoon honey
½ teaspoon olive oil

**NUTRITIONAL ANALYSIS**
(per serving):

Calories: 47
Protein: 6 g
Carbohydrate: 2 g
Fat: 2 g
Sat. Fat: 1 g
Cholesterol: 14 mg
Sodium: 20 mg
Fiber: trace
Exchange Approx.:
1 Lean Meat

# The Ultimate Grilled Cheeseburger Sandwich

**Serves 4**

1 tablespoon olive oil
1 teaspoon butter
2 thick slices of 7-Grain Bread
(see page 167)
1 ounce Cheddar cheese
½ pound (8 ounces) ground
round
Fresh minced garlic to taste
Balsamic vinegar to taste
Worcestershire sauce (see
Homemade recipe, page
17) to taste
Toppings of your choice, such
as stone-ground mustard,
mayonnaise, and so on

---

**NUTRITIONAL ANALYSIS**
(per serving):

Calories: 262
Protein: 17 g
Carbohydrate: 15 g
Fat: 15 g
Sat. Fat: 5 g
Cholesterol: 60 mg
Sodium: 187 mg
Fiber: 1 g
Exchange Approx.:
2 Lean Meats, 1 Fat,
1 Bread/Starch

1. Preheat your indoor grill. Combine the olive oil and butter, then use half of the mixture to "butter" 1 side of each slice of bread. Place the Cheddar cheese on the unbuttered side of 1 slice of bread and top with the other slice, buttered side up.

2. Combine the ground round with the Worcestershire sauce, garlic, and balsamic vinegar, if using. Shape the ground round into a large, rectangular patty, a little larger than a slice of the bread. Grill the patty and then the cheese sandwich. (If you are using a large indoor grill, position the hamburger at the lower end, near the area where the fat drains; grill the cheese sandwich at the higher end.)

3. Once the cheese sandwich is done, separate the slices of bread, being careful not to burn yourself on the cheese. Top 1 slice with the hamburger and add your choice of condiments and fixin's. Cut into quarters and serve.

## The Olive Oil Factor

Once you've used an olive oil and butter mixture to "butter" the bread for a toasted or grilled sandwich, you'll never want to use just plain butter again! The olive oil helps make the bread crunchier and imparts a subtle taste difference to the sandwich as well.

# Kovbasa (Ukrainian Kielbasa)

1. To prepare the peperivka, put 1 teaspoon of bourbon in a microwave-safe bowl and add a pinch of dried red pepper flakes. Microwave on high for 15 seconds, or until the mixture is hot. Set aside to cool.

2. Remove all the fat from the meat. Cut the meat into cubes, put them in a food processor and grind to desired consistency. Add all the remaining ingredients, including the cooled peperivka, and mix until well blended. The traditional preparation method calls for putting the sausage mixture in casings; however, it works equally well when broiled or grilled as fresh sausage patties.

**Yields 1½ pounds (24 ounces)**
**Serving size: 1 ounce**

1 pound (16 ounces) pork shoulder
½ pound (8 ounces) beef chuck
1 teaspoon freshly ground black pepper
½ teaspoon ground allspice
1 teaspoon garlic powder
1 teaspoon peperivka (spiced whiskey; see step 1)
Kosher or sea salt to taste (optional)

---

**NUTRITIONAL ANALYSIS**
(per serving):

Calories: 70
Protein: 8 g
Carbohydrate: 0 g
Fat: 4 g
Sat. Fat: 2 g
Cholesterol: 25 mg
Sodium: 15 mg
Fiber: 0 g
Exchange Approx.:
1 Medium-Fat Meat

# Italian Sausage

**Yields about 2 pounds
(32 ounces)
Serving size: 1 ounce**

2 pounds (32 ounces) pork
 shoulder
1 teaspoon ground black
 pepper
1 teaspoon dried parsley
1 teaspoon Italian-style
 seasoning
1 teaspoon garlic powder
¾ teaspoon crushed anise
 seeds
⅛ teaspoon crushed red
 pepper flakes
½ teaspoon paprika
½ teaspoon instant minced
 onion flakes
1 teaspoon kosher or sea salt
 (optional)

---

**NUTRITIONAL ANALYSIS**
(per serving, without salt):

Calories: 68
Protein: 8 g
Carbohydrate: 0 g
Fat: 4 g
Sat. Fat: 1 g
Cholesterol: 23 mg
Sodium: 14 mg
Fiber: 0 g
Exchange Approx.:
1 Medium-Fat Meat

1. Remove all fat from the meat. Cut the meat into cubes, put them in a food processor, and grind to desired consistency.

2. Add the remaining ingredients and mix until well blended. You can put the sausage mixture in casings, but it works equally well broiled or grilled as patties.

## Simple (and Smart!) Substitutions

Game meats—buffalo, venison, elk, moose—are low in fat, as are ground chicken or turkey. Substitute one of those meats for the pork in any of the sausage recipes in this chapter.

# Mock Chorizo

1. Remove all fat from the meat. Cut the meat into cubes, put them in a food processor, and grind to desired consistency. Add the remaining ingredients and mix until well blended.

2. Tradition calls for aging this sausage in an airtight container in the refrigerator for 4 days before cooking. Leftover sausage can be stored in the freezer for up to 3 months.

## Break from Tradition

Traditionally, chorizo is very high in fat. The chorizo recipes in this chapter are lower-fat alternatives. They make excellent replacements for adding flavor to recipes that call for bacon. In fact, 1 or 2 ounces of chorizo can replace an entire pound of bacon in cabbage, bean, or potato soup.

**Yields about 2 pounds
(32 ounces)**
**Serving size: 1 ounce**

2 pounds (32 ounces) lean
  pork
4 tablespoons chili powder
¼ teaspoon ground cloves
2 tablespoons paprika
2½ teaspoons crushed fresh
  garlic
1 teaspoon crushed, dried
  oregano
3½ tablespoons cider vinegar
1 teaspoon kosher or sea salt
  (optional)

---

**NUTRITIONAL ANALYSIS**
(per serving, without salt):

Calories: 68
Protein: 8 g
Carbohydrate: trace
Fat: 4 g
Sat. Fat: 1 g
Cholesterol: 23 mg
Sodium: 14 mg
Fiber: 0 g
Exchange Approx.:
1 Medium-Fat Meat

# Cinnamon Grilled Pork Tenderloin

**Serves 2**

2 teaspoons Bragg's Liquid Aminos
2 teaspoons burgundy or red wine
½ teaspoon honey
⅛ teaspoon garlic powder
⅛ teaspoon ground cinnamon
¼-pound (4-ounce) pork loin

---

**NUTRITIONAL ANALYSIS**
(per serving):

Calories: 104
Protein: 8 g
Carbohydrate: 4 g
Fat: 6 g
Sat. Fat: 2 g
Cholesterol: 20 mg
Sodium: 387 mg
Fiber: 0 g
Exchange Approx.:
2 Lean Meats

1. Combine the first 5 ingredients in a large zip-top plastic bag. Add the roast and marinate in the refrigerator for at least 1 hour, or up to 6 hours.

2. Grill tenderloins over hot coals until the thermometer reaches 160°F, turning while grilling. (Grilling time will depend on the thickness of the tenderloin. For example, a ¾" cut of pork grilled over medium-hot coals will take 12 to 14 minutes while a cut twice as thick, or a 1½" cut, can take more than half an hour.)

3. Allow the meat to rest for up to 15 minutes, then slice thinly against the grain.

## Let It Set!

Avoid the biggest cause of a dry roast! When you remove a roast from the oven, always allow it to rest for 10 minutes before you carve it. This allows the juices to redistribute through the roast (instead of draining out all over your cutting board).

# Fruited Pork Loin Roast Casserole

1. Preheat oven to 350°F (325°F if using a glass casserole dish) and treat a casserole dish with nonstick spray.

2. Layer half of the potato slices across the bottom of the dish. Top with 1 piece of the flattened pork loin. Arrange the apple slices over the top of the loin and place the apricot halves on top of the apple. Sprinkle the red onion (or shallots) over the apricot and apples. Add the second flattened pork loin and layer the remaining potatoes atop the loin. Drizzle the apple cider (or apple juice) over the top of the casserole.

3. Cover and bake for 45 minutes to 1 hour, or until the potatoes are tender. Keep the casserole covered to let it set for 10 minutes after you remove it from the oven.

*TIP: To enhance the flavor of this dish, you can top it with the optional ingredients when it's served. Just be sure to make the appropriate Exchange Approximations adjustments if you do.*

## Versatile Herbs

For a change of pace, you can substitute rosemary when thyme is called for in pork recipes.

**Serves 4**

4 small Yukon Gold potatoes, peeled and sliced
2 (2-ounce) pieces trimmed boneless pork loin, pounded flat
1 apple, peeled, cored, and sliced
4 apricot halves
1 tablespoon chopped red onion or shallot
⅛ cup apple cider or apple juice
Optional seasonings to taste:
Olive oil
Parmesan cheese
Salt and freshly ground pepper

**NUTRITIONAL ANALYSIS**
(per serving):

Calories: 170
Protein: 7 g
Carbohydrate: 27 g
Fat: 4 g
Sat. Fat: 1 g
Cholesterol: 19 mg
Sodium: 32 mg
Fiber: 3 g
Exchange Approx.:
1 Lean Meat, 1 Fruit, 1 Starch

# White Wine and Lemon Pork Roast

**Serves 4**

1 clove garlic, crushed
½ cup dry white wine
1 tablespoon lemon juice
1 teaspoon olive oil
1 tablespoon minced red onion or shallots
¼ teaspoon dried thyme
⅛ teaspoon ground black pepper
½-pound (8-ounce) pork loin roast

---

**NUTRITIONAL ANALYSIS**
(per serving):

Calories: 115
Protein: 12 g
Carbohydrate: 1 g
Fat: 4 g
Sat. Fat: 1 g
Cholesterol: 33 mg
Sodium: 31 mg
Fiber: trace
Exchange Approx.:
2 Lean Meats

1. Make the marinade by combining the first 7 ingredients in a heavy, freezer-style plastic bag. Add the roast and marinate in the refrigerator for an hour or overnight, according to taste. (Note: Pork loin is already tender, so you're marinating the meat to impart the flavors only.)

2. Preheat oven to 350°F. Remove meat from marinade and put on a nonstick spray–treated rack in a roasting pan. Roast for 20 to 30 minutes, or until the meat thermometer reads 150°F to 170°F, depending on how well done you prefer it.

## Marmalade Marinade

Combine 1 teaspoon Dijon or stone-ground mustard, 1 tablespoon sugar-free orange marmalade, 1 clove crushed garlic, and ¼ teaspoon dried thyme leaves. Marinate and prepare ½-pound (8-ounce) pork loin as you would the White Wine and Lemon Pork Loin Roast. The Nutritional Analysis for a 2-ounce serving is: Calories: 89; Protein: 9 g; Carbohydrate: 2 g; Fat: 5 g; Sat. Fat: 2 g; Cholesterol: 28 mg; Sodium: 41 mg; Fiber: trace; PCF Ratio: 57-9-34. Exchange Approximations: 2 Lean Meats

# Pecan-Crusted Roast Pork Loin

1. Put the olive oil, crushed garlic, honey, and seasonings (if using) in a heavy, freezer-style plastic bag. Work the bag until the ingredients are mixed. Add the roast and turn it in the bag to coat the meat. Marinate in the refrigerator for several hours or overnight.

2. Preheat oven to 400°F. Roll the pork loin in the chopped pecans and place it in a roasting pan. Make a tent of aluminum foil and arrange it over the pork loin, covering the nuts completely so that they won't char. Roast for 10 minutes, then lower the heat to 350°F. Continue to roast for another 8 to 15 minutes, or until the meat thermometer reads 150°F to 170°F, depending on how well done you prefer it.

## Create a Celery Roasting Rack

If you prefer to bake a loin roast in a casserole alongside potatoes and carrots, elevate the roast on 2 or 3 stalks of celery. The celery will absorb any fat that drains from the meat so that it's not absorbed by the other vegetables. Discard the celery.

**Serves 4**

1 teaspoon olive oil
1 clove garlic, crushed
1 teaspoon honey
Thyme, sage, and pepper to taste (optional)
¼ cup chopped or ground pecans
½-pound (8-ounce) boneless pork loin roast

**NUTRITIONAL ANALYSIS**
(per serving):

Calories: 132
Protein: 11 g
Carbohydrate: 3 g
Fat: 9 g
Sat. Fat: 1 g
Cholesterol: 26 mg
Sodium: 21 mg
Fiber: 1 g
Exchange Approx.:
2 Lean Meats, 1 Fat

# Main Dish Pork and Beans

**Serves 4**

1⅓ cups cooked pinto beans
2 tablespoons ketchup
¼ teaspoon Dijon mustard
¼ teaspoon dry mustard
1 teaspoon cider vinegar
4 tablespoons diced red onion
1 tablespoon sugar-free maple
   syrup
¼ pound (4 ounces) slow-
   cooked, shredded pork
⅛ cup (2 tablespoons) apple
   juice or cider

---

**NUTRITIONAL ANALYSIS**
(per serving):

Calories: 132
Protein: 10 g
Carbohydrate: 20 g
Fat: 2 g
Sat. Fat: trace
Cholesterol: 13 mg
Sodium: 119 mg
Fiber: 5 g
Exchange Approx.:
2 Lean Meats, ½ Free,
½ Fruit/Misc. Carb.

1. Preheat oven to 350°F.

2. In a casserole dish treated with nonstick spray, combine the first 7 ingredients. Layer the meat over the top of the bean mixture. Pour the apple juice (or cider) over the pork.

3. Bake for 20 to 30 minutes, or until the mixture is well heated and bubbling. Stir well before serving.

*TIP: If you prefer thicker baked beans, after cooking, remove some of the beans and mash them. Stir them back into the dish.*

## Pork Broth

For about 3 cups of broth, cook 1 pound lean pork shoulder or loin (cut into pieces) with 1 onion, 2 carrots, and 2 celery stalks (all chopped); 4 sprigs parsley, 6 peppercorns, ¼ cup white wine, and 4¾ cups water in a slow cooker. Use the high setting until mixture reaches a boil, then reduce heat to low. Allow to simmer overnight or up to 16 hours. Remove the pork, discard the vegetables, skim the fat, and freeze any broth you won't be using within a few days.

# Ham and Artichoke Hearts Scalloped Potatoes

1. Preheat oven to 300°F. Thaw the artichoke hearts and pat them dry with a paper towel. In a deep casserole dish treated with nonstick spray, layer the artichokes, onion, and potatoes, and lightly sprinkle salt and pepper over the top (if using).

2. In a food processor or blender, combine the lemon juice, wine, Mock Cream, cottage cheese, parsley, garlic powder, and Parmesan cheese, and process until smooth. Pour over the layered vegetables. Top with the ham. Cover the casserole dish (with a lid or foil) and bake for 35 to 40 minutes, or until the potatoes are cooked through.

3. Remove the cover and top with the Cheddar cheese. Return to the oven for another 10 minutes, or until the cheese is melted and bubbly. Let rest 10 minutes before cutting.

*TIP: If you are on a sodium-restricted diet, use 4 ounces of one of the cooked sausage recipes in this chapter in place of the ham. Adjust the Exchange Approximations from 1 Lean Meat to 1 Medium-Fat Meat.*

## Simple Substitutions

Artichoke hearts are expensive. You can substitute cabbage, broccoli, or cauliflower (or a mixture of all three) for the artichokes.

**Serves 4**

2 cups frozen artichoke hearts
1 cup chopped onion
4 small potatoes, thinly sliced
Sea salt and freshly ground black pepper to taste (optional)
1 tablespoon lemon juice
1 tablespoon dry white wine
1 cup Mock Cream (see page 20)
½ cup nonfat cottage cheese
1 teaspoon dried parsley
1 teaspoon garlic powder
⅛ cup freshly grated Parmesan cheese
¼ pound (4 ounces) lean ham, cubed
2 ounces Cheddar cheese, grated (to yield ½ cup)

**NUTRITIONAL ANALYSIS**
(per serving, without salt):

Calories: 269
Protein: 21 g
Carbohydrate: 31 g
Fat: 8 g
Sat. Fat: 4 g
Cholesterol: 28 mg
Sodium: 762 mg
Fiber: 6 g
Exchange Approx.:
1½ Lean Meats, ½ High-Fat Meat, 1½ Vegetables, 1 Starch

# Slow-Cooked Venison

**Yields about 1 pound**
**Serving size: 1 ounce**

1 pound venison roast
1–2 tablespoons cider vinegar

---

### NUTRITIONAL ANALYSIS
(per serving):

Calories: 45
Protein: 9 g
Carbohydrate: 0 g
Fat: 1 g
Sat. Fat: trace
Cholesterol: 32 mg
Sodium: 15 mg
Fiber: 0 g
Exchange Approx.:
1 Very Lean Meat

1. Put the venison into a ceramic-lined slow cooker, add enough water to cover, and add the vinegar; set on high. Once the mixture begins to boil, reduce temperature to low. Allow the meat to simmer for 8 or more hours.

2. Drain the resulting broth from the meat and discard it. Remove any remaining fat from the meat and discard that as well. Weigh the meat and separate it into servings. The meat will keep for 1 or 2 days in the refrigerator, or freeze portions for use later.

## Use Quality Equipment

Slow cookers with a ceramic interior maintain low temperatures better than do those with a metal cooking surface.

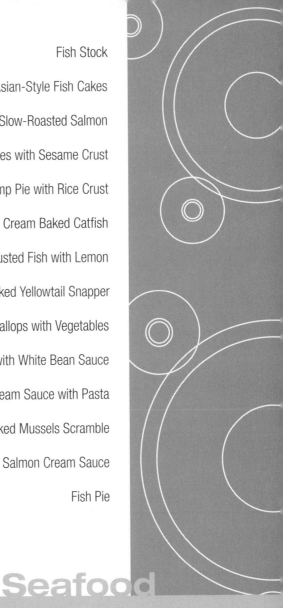

# Seafood

chapter six

# Fish Stock

**Yields 4 cups**
**Serving size: 1 cup**

4 cups fish heads, bones,
   and trimmings (approx. 1
   pound)
2 stalks celery and leaves,
   chopped
1 onion, chopped
1 carrot, peeled and chopped
1 bay leaf
4 sprigs fresh parsley
Sea salt and pepper to taste
   (optional)

## NUTRITIONAL ANALYSIS

(per serving):

Calories: 40
Protein: 5 g
Carbohydrate: 0 g
Fat: 2 g
Sat. Fat: trace
Cholesterol: 2 mg
Sodium: variable
Fiber: 0 g
Exchange Approx.:
1 Very Lean Meat

1. Use your own fish trimmings (saved in a bag in the freezer), or ask the butcher at your local fish market or supermarket for fish trimmings. Wash the trimmings well.

2. In a stockpot, combine all the ingredients and add enough water to cover everything by an inch or so. Bring to a boil over high heat, then reduce heat to low. Skim off the foam that rises to the top. Cover and simmer for 20 minutes.

3. Remove from the heat and strain through a sieve, discarding all solids. Refrigerate or freeze.

*Tip: To make stock from shellfish, simply sub-stitute shrimp, crab, or lobster shells for the fish heads and bones.*

## Proper Fish Handling

Always wash your hands after handling raw fish, and wash all surfaces and utensils that the raw fish touched.

# Asian-Style Fish Cakes

1. Preheat oven to 375°F. Cut the fish into 1-inch pieces and combine with the green onions, banana pepper, garlic, ginger, Bragg's Liquid Aminos, lemon juice, and lemon zest in a food processor. Process until chopped and mixed. (You do not want to purée this mixture; it should be a rough chop.) Add the Old Bay Seasoning, if using, and stir to mix.

2. Form the fish mixture into patties of about 2 tablespoons each; you should have 16 patties total. Place the patties on a baking sheet treated with nonstick cooking spray, and bake for 12 to 15 minutes, or until crisp. (Alternatively, you can fry these in a nonstick pan for about 4 minutes on each side.)

*TIP: For crunchy fish cakes, coat each side in the rice flour and then lightly spritz the top of the patties with the olive or peanut oil before baking as directed.*

## Not All Weeds Are Bad

Seaweed is an important ingredient in many processed foods, such as commercial ice cream and other foods that contain carrageenan, a thickener found in several kinds of seaweed.

**Serves 8**

1 pound catfish fillet
2 green onions, minced
1 banana pepper, cored, seeded, and chopped
2 cloves garlic, minced
1 tablespoon grated or minced ginger
1 tablespoon Bragg's Liquid Aminos
1 tablespoon lemon juice
1 teaspoon lemon zest
Optional seasonings to taste: Rice flour, olive or peanut oil, Old Bay

**NUTRITIONAL ANALYSIS**
(per serving):

Calories: 66
Protein: 11 g
Carbohydrate: 1 g
Fat: 2 g
Sat. Fat: trace
Cholesterol: 41 mg
Sodium: 112 mg
Fiber: trace
PCF Ratio: 69-8-23
Exchange Approx.:
1 Lean Meat, 1 Free Condiment

# Slow-Roasted Salmon

**Serves 4**

4 (5-ounce) salmon fillets with skin, at room temperature
2 teaspoons extra-virgin olive oil
1 cup finely minced fresh chives
Sea or kosher salt and freshly ground white pepper to taste (optional)
Sage sprigs, for garnish

---

**NUTRITIONAL ANALYSIS**
(per serving):

Calories: 257
Protein: 25 g
Carbohydrate: trace
Fat: 16 g
Sat. Fat: 3 g
Cholesterol: 71 mg
Sodium: 69 mg
Fiber: trace
Exchange Approx.:
4 Lean Meats, ½ Fat

1. Preheat oven to 250°F. Rub ½ teaspoon of the olive oil into the flesh side of each salmon fillet. Completely cover the fillets with the chives and gently press them into the flesh. Season with salt and white pepper, if desired.

2. Place the fillets skin-side down on a non-stick, oven-safe skillet or a foil-lined cookie sheet treated with nonstick spray, and roast for 25 minutes.

# Crab Cakes with Sesame Crust

1. Preheat oven to 375°F. In a large bowl, mix together the crab, egg, ginger, scallion, sherry, lemon juice, mayonnaise, and the seasonings, if using.

2. Form the mixture into 10 equal cakes. Spread the sesame seeds over a sheet pan and dip both sides of the cakes to coat them. Arrange the crab cakes on a baking sheet treated with nonstick spray. Typical baking time is 8 to 10 minutes (depending on how thick you make the cakes).

## So, What Is Aquaculture?

"Aquaculture produces about 17 percent of the world's seafood. . . . Seaweed cultivation ranks first in volume, followed by carp, and blue mussels. In the U.S., catfish is the predominant farmed species, followed by trout, salmon, and shellfish." (Source: Ducktrap River Fish Farm's Aquaculture FAQ page at *www.ducktrap.com*)

**Serves 5**

1 pound (16 ounces) lump crabmeat
1 egg
1 tablespoon minced fresh ginger
1 small scallion, finely chopped
1 tablespoon dry sherry
1 tablespoon freshly squeezed lemon juice
6 tablespoons Hellmann's or Best Foods Real Mayonnaise
Sea salt and freshly ground white pepper to taste (optional)
¼ cup lightly toasted sesame seeds

**NUTRITIONAL ANALYSIS**
(per serving):

Calories: 108
Protein: 9 g
Carbohydrate: 3 g
Fat: 6 g
Sat. Fat: 1 g
Cholesterol: 45 mg
Sodium: 171 mg
Fiber: 1 g
Exchange Approx.:
1 Very Lean Meat,
1½ Fats

# Creamy Shrimp Pie with Rice Crust

**Serves 4**

1⅓ cups cooked white rice
2 teaspoons dried parsley
2 tablespoons grated onion
1 teaspoon olive oil
1 tablespoon butter
1 clove garlic, crushed
1 pound shrimp, peeled and
  deveined
1 recipe Condensed Cream
  of Mushroom Soup (see
  page 60)
1 teaspoon lemon juice
1 cup sliced mushrooms,
  steamed

---

**NUTRITIONAL ANALYSIS**

(per serving):

Calories: 273
Protein: 26 g
Carbohydrate: 27 g
Fat: 6 g
Sat. Fat: 2 g
Cholesterol: 180 mg
Sodium: 172 mg
Fiber: 2 g
Exchange Approx.:
2 Very Lean Meats,
2 Starches, 1 Fat

1. Preheat oven to 350°F. Combine the cooked rice, parsley, and onion; mix well. Use the olive oil to coat a 10-inch pie plate. Press the rice mixture evenly around the sides and bottom. This works best if the rice is moist; if necessary, add 1 teaspoon of water.

2. Melt the butter in a deep, nonstick skillet over medium heat and sauté the garlic. Add the shrimp and cook, stirring frequently, until pink, about 5 minutes. Add the soup and lemon juice to the skillet. Stir until smooth and thoroughly heated. (If the soup seems too thick, add some water, 1 teaspoon at a time.) Stir the mushrooms into the soup mixture, then pour it over the rice "crust." Bake for 30 minutes, or until lightly browned on top. Serve hot.

## Fat-Free Flavor

To add the flavor of sautéed mushrooms or onions without the added fat of butter or oil, roast or grill them first. Simply spread them on a baking sheet treated with nonstick spray. Roasting them for 5 minutes in a 350°F oven will be sufficient if the vegetables are sliced, and will not add additional cooking time to the recipe.

# Mock Sour Cream
# Baked Catfish

1. Preheat oven to 350°F. Prepare a baking dish by spraying it with nonstick spray. Rinse the fillets in water and then dry between layers of paper towels. Arrange the fillets in the baking dish.

2. In a small bowl, combine the mayonnaise, flour, yogurt, vinegar, olives, celery seed, paprika, pepper, and thyme; spread the mixture over the fish and sprinkle with dill. Bake for 15 minutes, or until the fish flakes when touched with a fork. Garnish with lemon wedges and parsley, if desired.

**Serves 4**

1 pound (16 ounces) catfish
fillets
2 teaspoons Hellmann's
or Best Foods Real
Mayonnaise
2 teaspoons all-purpose flour
½ cup plain nonfat yogurt
½ teaspoon white wine
vinegar
4 teaspoons chopped
pimiento-stuffed green
olives
½ teaspoon ground celery
seed
¼ teaspoon paprika
¼ teaspoon freshly ground
white or black pepper
¼ teaspoon thyme
1 teaspoon fresh dill (or a
pinch of dried dill per fillet)
1 lemon, cut into 4 wedges
(optional)
Fresh chopped or dried
parsley (optional)

**NUTRITIONAL ANALYSIS**
(per serving):

Calories: 171
Protein: 18 g
Carbohydrate: 2 g
Fat: 10 g
Sat. Fat: 2 g
Cholesterol: 54 mg
Sodium: 102 mg
Fiber: trace
Exchange Approx.:
3 Lean Meats

# Baked Bread Crumb–Crusted Fish with Lemon

**Serves 6**

2 large lemons
1½ pounds (24 ounces)
   halibut fillets
¼ cup dried bread crumbs
Sea or kosher salt and freshly
   ground white or black
   pepper to taste (optional)

---

**NUTRITIONAL ANALYSIS**
(per serving, without salt):

Calories: 137
Protein: 24 g
Carbohydrate: 5 g
Fat: 3 g
Sat. Fat: trace
Cholesterol: 36 mg
Sodium: 73 mg
Fiber: 2 g
Exchange Approx.:
2 Very Lean Meats,
½ Starch, ½ Free
Condiment

1. Preheat oven to 375°F. Wash 1 lemon and cut it into thin slices. Grate 1 tablespoon of zest from the second lemon, then juice it. Combine the grated zest and bread crumbs in a small bowl and stir to mix; set aside.

2. Put the lemon juice in a shallow dish, and arrange the lemon slices in the bottom of a baking dish treated with nonstick spray. Dip the fish pieces in the lemon juice and set them on the lemon slices in the baking dish. Sprinkle the bread crumb mixture evenly over the fish pieces, along with the salt and pepper, if using, and bake until the crumbs are lightly browned and the fish is just opaque, 10 to 15 minutes. (Baking time will depend on the thickness of the fish.) Serve immediately, using the lemon slices as garnish.

## Lemon Infusion

Mildly flavored fish, such as catfish, cod, halibut, orange roughy, rockfish, and snapper, benefit from the distinctive flavor of lemon. Adding slices of lemon to the top of the fish allows the flavor to infuse into the fish.

# Sweet Onion–Baked Yellowtail Snapper

1. In a covered, microwave-safe dish, microwave the onion on high for 5 minutes, or until it is transparent. Carefully remove the cover and stir in the vinegar and honey. Cover and allow to set for several minutes so the onion absorbs the flavors.

2. Heat a nonstick pan on medium-high and add the olive oil. Transfer the steamed onion mixture to the pan and sauté until browned but not crisp. (Be careful as the onions will burn easily because of the honey; if the onion browns too quickly, lower the heat and add a few tablespoons of water.) Cook until all liquid has evaporated from the pan, stirring often. The onions should have a shiny and dark caramelized color. (This can be prepared 2 to 3 days in advance; store tightly covered in the refrigerator.)

3. Preheat oven to 375°F. Rinse the snapper fillets in cold water and dry between paper towels. Arrange the fillets on a baking sheet treated with nonstick spray. Spoon the caramelized onions over the tops of the fillets, pressing it to form a light "crust" over the top of the fish. Bake for 12 to 15 minutes, or until the fish flakes easily with a fork. Serve immediately with Madeira sauce divided on 4 plates with the fish placed on top.

**Serves 4**

2 cups sliced Vidalia onions
1 tablespoon balsamic vinegar
2 teaspoons honey
4 teaspoons olive oil
1 pound (16 ounces) skinless yellowtail snapper fillets
Sea salt and freshly ground white or black pepper to taste (optional)
Madeira Sauce (page 23)

**NUTRITIONAL ANALYSIS**
(per serving, no salt):

Calories: 185
Protein: 24 g
Carbohydrate: 8 g
Fat: 6 g
Sat. Fat: 1 g
Cholesterol: 42 mg
Sodium: 139 mg
Fiber: 1 g
Exchange Approx.:
1 Lean Meat, 2 Very Lean Meats, 1 Vegetable, ½ Starch

# Stir-Fried Ginger Scallops with Vegetables

**Serves 4**

1 pound (16 ounces) scallops
1 teaspoon peanut or sesame oil
1 tablespoon chopped fresh ginger
2 cloves garlic, minced
1 teaspoon rice wine vinegar
2 teaspoons Bragg's Liquid Aminos
½ cup low-fat, reduced-sodium chicken broth
2 cups broccoli florets
4 scallions, thinly sliced (optional)
1 teaspoon cornstarch
¼ teaspoon toasted sesame oil

**NUTRITIONAL ANALYSIS**
(per serving):

Calories: 145
Protein: 22 g
Carbohydrate: 8 g
Fat: 3 g
Sat. Fat: trace
Cholesterol: 37 mg
Sodium: 373 mg
Fiber: 2 g
Exchange Approx.:
3 Very Lean Meats,
½ Vegetable

1. Rinse the scallops and pat them dry between layers of paper towels. If necessary, slice the scallops so they're a uniform size. Set aside.

2. Add the peanut oil to a heated nonstick deep skillet or wok. Sauté the ginger and garlic for 1 to 2 minutes, being careful that the ginger doesn't burn. Add the vinegar, Liquid Aminos, and broth, and bring to a boil. Remove from heat.

3. Place the broccoli in a large, covered microwave-safe dish and pour the chicken broth mixture over the top. Microwave on high for 3 to 5 minutes, depending on how you prefer your vegetables cooked.

4. Heat the skillet or wok over medium-high temperature. Add the scallops and sauté for 1 minute on each side. (Do the scallops in batches if necessary. Be careful not to overcook the scallops.) Remove the scallops from pan when done and set aside. Drain off (but do not discard) the liquid from the broccoli; return the liquid to the bowl and transfer the broccoli to the heated skillet or wok. Stir-fry the vegetables to bring them up to serving temperature.

5. In the meantime, in a small cup or bowl, add enough water to the cornstarch to make a slurry, or roux. Whisk the slurry into the reserved broccoli liquid; microwave on high for 1 minute. Add the toasted sesame oil to the broth mixture, then whisk again. Pour the thickened broth mixture over the broccoli and toss to mix. Add the scallops back to the broccoli mixture and stir-fry over medium heat to return the scallops to serving temperature. Serve over rice or pasta topped with optional scallions, and adjust Exchange Approximations accordingly.

# Scallops and Shrimp with White Bean Sauce

1. In a nonstick saucepan, sauté the onion and garlic in 1 teaspoon of the oil over moderately low heat until the onion is soft. Add the wine and simmer the mixture until the wine is reduced by half. Add the parsley, basil, ⅓ cup of the beans, and the chicken broth; simmer the mixture, stirring constantly, for 1 minute.

2. Transfer the bean mixture to a blender or food processor and purée it. Pour the purée back into the saucepan and add the remaining beans; simmer for 2 minutes.

3. In a nonstick skillet, heat the remaining 1 teaspoon of oil over moderately high heat until it is hot but not smoking. Sauté the shrimp for 2 minutes on each side, or until they are cooked through. Using a slotted spoon, transfer the shrimp to a plate and cover to keep warm. Add the scallops to the skillet and sauté them for 1 minute on each side, or until they are cooked through. To serve, divide the bean sauce between 4 shallow bowls and arrange the shellfish over the top.

**Serves 4**

½ cup finely chopped onion, steamed
2 cloves garlic, minced
2 teaspoons olive oil, divided
¼ cup dry white wine
¼ cup, tightly packed, fresh parsley leaves
¼ cup, tightly packed, fresh basil leaves
1⅓ cups canned cannellini (white) beans, drained and rinsed
¼ cup low-fat, reduced-sodium chicken broth
½ pound (8 ounces) shrimp, shelled and deveined
½ pound (8 ounces) scallops

**NUTRITIONAL ANALYSIS**
(per serving):

Calories: 231
Protein: 27 g
Carbohydrate: 18 g
Fat: 4 g
Sat. Fat: 1 g
Cholesterol: 105 mg
Sodium: 217 mg
Fiber: 6 g
Exchange Approx.:
3 Very Lean Meats,
½ Fat, 1 Starch, ½ Vegetable

# Smoked Mussels in Cream Sauce with Pasta

**Serves 4**

2 teaspoons unsalted butter
2 cloves garlic, crushed
½ cup sliced leeks or green onions
½ cup dry white wine
2 cups steamed, sliced mushrooms
1⅓ cups uncooked pasta (to yield 2 cups cooked)
2 cups nonfat cottage cheese
1 teaspoon potato flour (optional)
4 ounces Ducktrap River smoked mussels, drained of any oil
2 teaspoons extra-virgin olive oil
Parsley to taste (optional)
Tarragon to taste (optional)
Cracked black or white pepper to taste (optional)

---

**NUTRITIONAL ANALYSIS**
(per serving, without flour):

Calories: 312
Protein: 22 g
Carbohydrate: 28 g
Fat: 10 g
Sat. Fat: 3 g
Cholesterol: 40 mg
Sodium: 362 mg
Fiber: 3 g
Exchange Approx.:
2 Very Lean Meats,
1 Lean Meat, 1 Fat,
1½ Carbs./Starches

1. Melt the butter in a deep nonstick skillet. Add the garlic and leeks (or green onions) and sauté just until transparent. Add the wine and bring to a boil; cook until reduced by half. Add the mushrooms and toss in the wine mixture. Start preparing the pasta according to package directions.

2. In a blender or food processor, purée the cottage cheese. Add it to the wine-mushroom mixture and bring to serving temperature over low heat, being careful that the mixture doesn't boil. If the mixture seems too wet (if you didn't reduce the wine enough, for example), sprinkle potato flour over the mixture, stir until blended, and cook until thickened.

3. Add the mussels to the cottage cheese mixture just prior to serving, stirring well to bring the mussels to serving temperature. Serve over the drained cooked pasta, tossed with the olive oil and the herbs, if using. Top with cracked pepper.

# Smoked Mussels Scramble

In a bowl, combine all the ingredients. "Fry" in a nonstick skillet sprayed with olive oil nonstick spray. You can prepare the scramble loose, or in patties.

*TIP: For patties, shape into balls, roll in rice flour (for extra crispness), place in skillet, and flatten with the back of a spatula. Because this is a very moist mixture, be sure to wet your hands before you shape it into balls.*

## Know Your Ingredients

Because smoked meats are also often high in sodium, most recipes in this book state the brand used so that the sodium counts given in the Nutritional Analysis are accurate. If you substitute another brand, consult the label and adjust the nutritional values, if necessary.

**Serves 4**

4 smoked mussels (1 ounce)
1 egg
1 tablespoon unbleached all-purpose flour
1 tablespoon cornmeal
1 tablespoon rice flour
1 tablespoon diced, sautéed celery
1 tablespoon diced, sautéed green pepper
2 tablespoons diced, sautéed onion
6 ounces (2 small) diced, boiled potatoes
Rice flour (optional)

**NUTRITIONAL ANALYSIS**
(per serving):

Calories: 93
Protein: 4 g
Carbohydrate: 13 g
Fat: 3 g
Sat. Fat: 1 g
Cholesterol: 54 mg
Sodium: 108 mg
Fiber: 2 g
Exchange Approx.:
1 Starch, ½ Very Lean Meat

# Smoked Salmon Cream Sauce

**Serves 4**

2 teaspoons butter
4 ounces Ducktrap River
    smoked salmon
2 cups nonfat cottage cheese
Ground nutmeg (optional)
Freshly ground white or black
    pepper (optional)

**NUTRITIONAL ANALYSIS**
(per serving, sauce only):

Calories: 143
Protein: 18 g
Carbohydrate: 1 g
Fat: 7 g
Sat. Fat: 3 g
Cholesterol: 15 mg
Sodium: 355 mg
Fiber: 0 g
Exchange Approx.:
3 Very Lean Meats,
½ Fat

1. Melt the butter in a nonstick skillet. Cut the smoked salmon into julienne strips, and sauté in the butter until heated through. In a blender or food processor, blend the cottage cheese until smooth.

2. Stir the puréed cottage cheese into the sautéed salmon and heat on low until the cottage cheese is brought to serving temperature. Spoon the sauce over 4 servings of cooked pasta or toast. Top with the nutmeg and pepper, if desired.

# Fish Pie

1. Preheat oven to 450°F. In a nonstick sauce-pan, heat the Mock Cream and bring it to a boil. Remove from the heat and add the cheeses, onion, lemon juice, mustard, parsley, and carrots. Press the steamed spinach between layers of paper towels to remove any excess moisture.

2. Mix together the spinach, smoked trout, cod, and egg; put into a baking dish treated with nonstick spray. Pour the cheese mixture over the fish mixture.

3. In a food processor, combine the steamed potatoes, olive oil, and seasonings (if using), and pulse until the potatoes are coarsely mashed. Spread the potatoes over the top of the fish mixture. Bake for 25 to 30 minutes, or until the potatoes are golden.

**Serves 4**

1 cup Mock Cream (page 20)
¼ cup grated, low-salt Cheddar cheese
1 tablespoon grated Parmesan cheese
¼ cup red or sweet onion, steamed
¼ cup lemon juice
1 teaspoon stone-ground mustard
1 teaspoon dried parsley
½ cup sliced carrot, steamed
1 cup, tightly packed, spinach
2 ounces Ducktrap River smoked trout, diced
1 pound skinless cod fillets, cut into 1-inch cubes
1 hard-boiled egg, grated or finely chopped
¾ pound potatoes, boiled (without salt) and diced
2 teaspoons extra-virgin olive oil

**NUTRITIONAL ANALYSIS**
(per serving, without salt):

Calories: 301
Protein: 33 g
Carbohydrate: 28 g
Fat: 7 g
Sat. Fat: 3 g
Cholesterol: 115 mg
Sodium: 331 mg
Fiber: 3 g
Exchange Approx.: 2 Very Lean Meats, 1 High-Fat Meat, 1 Carb./Starch, ½ Vegetable, ½ Skim Milk

# Pasta and Pizza

## chapter seven

# Quick Tomato Sauce

**Serves 8**

2 pounds very ripe tomatoes
2 tablespoons extra-virgin
    olive oil
2 cloves garlic, minced
½ teaspoon ground cumin
2 large sprigs fresh thyme, or
    ½ teaspoon dried thyme
1 bay leaf
Kosher or sea salt and freshly
    ground black pepper to
    taste (optional)
3 tablespoons total of
    chopped fresh basil,
    oregano, tarragon, and
    parsley or cilantro; or, a
    combination of all the listed
    herbs according to taste. If
    using dried herbs, reduce
    the amount to 1 tablespoon

---

**NUTRITIONAL ANALYSIS**
(per serving, without salt):

Calories: 40
Protein: 1 g
Carbohydrate: 6 g
Fat: 2 g
Sat. Fat: trace
Cholesterol: 0 mg
Sodium: 10 mg
Fiber: 1 g
Exchange Approx.:
1 Vegetable, ½ Fat

1. Peel and seed the tomatoes; chop them with a knife or food processor.

2. Heat a large skillet and add the olive oil. Reduce the heat to low and sauté the garlic and cumin. Add the tomatoes, thyme, bay leaf, salt and pepper, if using. If you are using dried herbs, add them now. Simmer, uncovered, over medium heat for 8 to 10 minutes, stirring often; reduce the heat to maintain a simmer, if necessary. Simmer until the tomatoes are soft and the sauce has thickened. Discard the bay leaf and thyme sprigs. Adjust the seasoning to taste. If you are using fresh herbs, add them just before serving. This sauce is delicious served hot or cold.

## Remember . . .

The addition of ¼ teaspoon of Splenda granular in tomato sauce helps cut the acidity of the tomatoes without affecting the Exchange Approximations for the recipe.

# Basic Tomato Sauce

1. Heat the olive oil in a large, deep skillet or saucepan over medium-high heat. Add the onions, carrots, and garlic; sauté until the onions are transparent. (For a richer-tasting sauce, allow the onions to caramelize or reach a light golden brown.) Purée the tomatoes in a food processor.

2. Add the tomatoes, herbs, and Splenda granular to the onion mixture along with the salt, pepper, and anise, if using. Simmer, partially covered, for 45 minutes. Process the sauce in the food processor again if you prefer a smoother sauce.

## Culinary Antacids

Stir in a 2 teaspoons of sugar-free grape jelly to tame hot chili or acidic sauce. You won't really notice the flavor of the jelly, and it will do a great job of reducing any tart, bitter, or acidic tastes in your sauce.

**Yields about 5 cups**
**Serving size: ¼ cup**

2 tablespoons olive oil
2 cups coarsely chopped
 yellow onion
½ cup sliced carrots
2 cloves garlic, minced
4 cups canned Italian plum
 tomatoes with juice
1 teaspoon dried oregano
1 teaspoon dried basil
¼ teaspoon Splenda granular
Kosher or sea salt and freshly
 ground black pepper to
 taste (optional)
Dash of ground anise seed
 (optional)

**NUTRITIONAL ANALYSIS**
(per serving, without salt):

Calories: 28
Protein: 1 g
Carbohydrate: 4 g
Fat: 2 g
Sat. Fat: trace
Cholesterol: 0 mg
Sodium: 17 mg
Fiber: 1 g
Exchange Approx.:
1½ Vegetables

# Uncooked Tomato Sauce

**Serves 4**

½ cup fresh basil leaves, divided
2 pounds firm ripe tomatoes, peeled, seeded, and chopped
2 cloves garlic, minced
4 tablespoons thinly sliced scallions (white and green parts)
2 tablespoons minced fresh parsley
4 teaspoons extra-virgin olive oil
1½ teaspoons red wine vinegar or lemon juice
¼ teaspoon Splenda granular
Kosher or sea salt and freshly ground black pepper to taste (optional)

---

### NUTRITIONAL ANALYSIS
(per serving, without salt):

Calories: 88
Protein: 2 g
Carbohydrate: 11 g
Fat: 5 g
Sat. Fat: 1 g
Cholesterol: 0 mg
Sodium: 80 mg
Fiber: 3 g
Exchange Approx.:
2 Vegetables, 1 Fat

1. Chop half the basil leaves and set the rest aside until later.

2. In a large bowl combine the chopped basil, tomatoes, garlic, scallions, parsley, olive oil, vinegar (or lemon juice), and Splenda. Let the mixture sit at room temperature for at least 4 hours, but no more than 6, then season with salt and pepper, if using. Garnish with the remaining basil.

## English Muffin Pizzas

Top each half of an English muffin with your choice of tomato sauce. Add chopped, free-choice vegetables. Divide 1 ounce of grated mozzarella cheese between the muffin halves. Bake in a 400°F oven until the cheese bubbles, and you have a meal with 2 Carbohydrate/ Starch Exchanges and 1 Medium-Fat Meat Exchange, plus the Exchange Approximation for your choice of sauce.

# Fusion Lo Mein

1. In a food processor or blender, combine the vinegar, pineapple juice, orange juice, shallots, lemon juice, cornstarch, Worcestershire, honey, and garlic; process until smooth.

2. Heat a wok or large nonstick skillet coated with cooking spray over medium-high heat until hot, then add the olive oil. Add the onions and stir-fry for 1 minute. Add the carrots, bell peppers, and broccoli, and stir-fry for another minute. Cover the pan and cook for 2 more minutes. Add the vinegar mixture and the sprouts. Bring the mixture to a boil and cook, uncovered, for 30 seconds, stirring constantly. Add the cooked pasta and toss to mix.

**Serves 6**

2 tablespoons rice vinegar
1 tablespoon pineapple juice
1 tablespoon orange juice
2 teaspoons minced shallots
2 teaspoons lemon juice
1 teaspoon cornstarch
1 teaspoon Worcestershire
    sauce (see recipe for
    Homemade on page 17)
1 teaspoon honey
2 cloves garlic, minced
1 teaspoon olive oil
¾ cup chopped green onions
1 cup diagonally sliced
    (¼-inch thick) carrots
1 cup julienned yellow bell
    pepper
1 cup julienned red bell pepper
3 cups small broccoli florets
1 cup fresh bean sprouts
1½ cups cooked pasta

**NUTRITIONAL ANALYSIS**
(per serving):

Calories: 155
Protein: 6 g
Carbohydrate: 31 g
Fat: 1 g
Sat. Fat: trace
Cholesterol: 0 mg
Sodium: 30 mg
Fiber: 3 g
Exchange Approx.:
1 Carb./Starch, 1 Veg-
etable, ½ Fruit

# Roasted Butternut Squash Pasta

**Serves 4**

1 butternut squash
4 teaspoons extra-virgin olive
    oil
1 clove garlic, minced
1 cup chopped red onion
2 teaspoons red wine vinegar
¼ teaspoon dried oregano
2 cups cooked pasta
Freshly ground black pepper
    (optional)

## NUTRITIONAL ANALYSIS

(per serving):

Calories: 217
Protein: 5 g
Carbohydrate: 40 g
Fat: 5 g
Sat. Fat: 1 g
Cholesterol: 0 mg
Sodium: 8 mg
Fiber: 2 g
Exchange Approx.:
1 Starch 1 Carb./
Starch, 1 Fat, ½ Vege-
table

1. Preheat oven to 400°F. Cut the squash in half and scoop out the seeds. Using nonstick spray, coat 1 side of each of 2 pieces of heavy-duty foil large enough to wrap the squash halves. Wrap the squash in the foil and place on a baking sheet; bake for 1 hour, or until tender.

2. Scoop out the baked squash flesh and discard the rind. Rough chop the squash. Add the olive oil, garlic, and onion to a nonstick skillet and sauté until the onion is transparent. (Alternatively, put the oil, garlic, and onion in a covered microwave-safe dish and microwave on high for 2 to 3 minutes.)

3. Remove pan from heat and stir in the vinegar and oregano. Add the squash and stir to coat it in the onion mixture. Add the pasta and toss to mix. Season with freshly ground black pepper, if desired.

*TIP: For added flavor, use roasted instead of raw garlic in this recipe. Roasting the garlic causes it to caramelize, adding a natural sweetness.*

# Pasta with Artichokes

1. Cook the artichokes in the water and lemon juice according to package directions; drain, reserving ¼ cup of the liquid. Cool the artichokes, then cut into quarters. (Alternatively, you can decrease the amount of water to 3 tablespoons and add it with the artichokes and lemon juice to a covered microwave-safe dish. Microwave according to package directions; reserve all of the liquid. This results in a stronger lemon flavor, which compensates for the lack of salt in this recipe.)

2. Heat the olive oil in a nonstick skillet over medium heat. Add the garlic and sauté for 1 minute. Reduce heat to low and stir in the artichokes and tomatoes; simmer for 1 minute. Stir in the reserved artichoke liquid, red pepper flakes, and parsley; simmer for 5 minutes. Pour the artichoke sauce over the pasta in a large bowl; toss gently to coat. Sprinkle with cheese and top with pepper, if desired.

## Garlic Toast

Large amounts of a butter- or olive oil–garlic mixture make garlic bread high in fat. For delicious results with only a touch of fat, spritz both sides of sliced bread with olive oil, and bake for 6 to 8 minutes in a 350°F oven. Handling the toasted bread slices carefully, rub a cut garlic clove across the top of each slice. Nutritional Analysis and Exchange Approximations depend on the size and choice of bread slices; if done properly, each slice will have only a trace of fat.

**Serves 4**

1 (10-ounce) package frozen artichoke hearts
1¼ cups water
1 tablespoon lemon juice
4 teaspoons olive oil
¼ cup sun-dried tomatoes, packed in oil (drained and chopped)
2 cloves garlic, minced
¼ teaspoon red pepper flakes
2 teaspoons dried parsley
2 cups cooked pasta
¼ cup grated Parmesan cheese
Freshly ground black pepper to taste (optional)

**NUTRITIONAL ANALYSIS** (per serving):

Calories: 308
Protein: 10 g
Carbohydrate: 47 g
Fat: 9 g
Sat. Fat: 2 g
Cholesterol: 2 mg
Sodium: 87 mg
Fiber: 3 g
Exchange Approx.:
1 Medium-Fat Meat,
2 Vegetables, 1 Carb./
Starch, 2 Fats

# Pasta with Creamed Clam Sauce

**Serves 4**

1 (6½-ounce) can chopped clams
4 teaspoons olive oil
1 clove garlic
1 tablespoon dry white wine or dry vermouth
½ cup Mock Cream (see page 20)
¼ cup freshly grated Parmesan cheese
2 cups cooked pasta
Freshly ground black pepper to taste (optional)

## NUTRITIONAL ANALYSIS

(per serving):

Calories: 226
Protein: 15 g
Carbohydrate: 24 g
Fat: 7 g
Sat. Fat: 2 g
Cholesterol: 25 mg
Sodium: 209 mg
Fiber: 1 g
Exchange Approx.:
1 Lean Meat, 1 Carb./ Starch, 1 Fat, ½ Skim Milk

1. Drain the canned clams and reserve the juice. Heat the olive oil in a large nonstick skillet. Add the garlic and sauté for 1 minute; stir in the clams and sauté for another minute. With a slotted spoon, transfer the clams to a bowl and cover to keep warm.

2. Add the wine (or vermouth) and reserved clam juice to the skillet, bring to a boil, and reduce by half. Lower the heat and add the Mock Cream and bring to serving temperature, being careful not to boil the cream. Stir in the Parmesan cheese and continue to heat the sauce for another minute, stirring constantly. Add the pasta and toss with the sauce. Divide into 4 equal servings and serve immediately, topped with freshly ground pepper, if desired.

# Pasta with Tuna Alfredo Sauce

1. Process the cottage cheese and skim milk together in a food processor or blender until smooth. Set aside.

2. Heat the olive oil in a large nonstick skillet. Add the garlic and sauté for 1 minute; stir in the tuna and sauté for another minute. Add the wine to the skillet and bring to a boil. Lower the heat and add the cottage cheese mixture and bring to serving temperature, being careful not to let it boil. Stir in the Parmesan cheese and continue to heat the sauce for 1 minute, stirring constantly. Add the pasta and toss with the sauce. Divide into 4 equal servings and serve immediately, topped with freshly ground pepper, if desired.

**Serves 4**

1 cup nonfat cottage cheese
1 tablespoon skim milk
2 teaspoons olive oil
1 clove garlic, minced
2 (6-ounce) cans tuna packed in water, drained
⅛ cup (2 tablespoons) dry white wine
¼ cup freshly grated Parmesan cheese
2 cups cooked pasta
Freshly ground black pepper to taste (optional)

---

**NUTRITIONAL ANALYSIS**
(per serving):

Calories: 278
Protein: 33 g
Carbohydrate: 21 g
Fat: 5 g
Sat. Fat: 2 g
Cholesterol: 32 mg
Sodium: 401 mg
Fiber: 1 g
Exchange Approx.:
1½ Very Lean Meats,
1½ Lean Meats, 1½
Carbs./Starches

# Pasta Fagioli

## Serves 8

1 (16-ounce) package ziti pasta
2 tablespoons olive oil
2 cloves garlic, minced
1½ cups sugar snap peas
1½ cups diced cooked extra-lean (4 percent) ham
1 (16-ounce) can cannellini beans, drained
¼ cup sun-dried tomatoes packed in oil, drained and chopped
1½ cups low-fat, reduced-sodium chicken broth
½ teaspoon kosher or sea salt
¼ teaspoon cracked black pepper
¼ cup grated Parmesan cheese

1. Cook the pasta as directed on the package. Meanwhile, heat a large skillet on medium and add the olive oil. Sauté the garlic for 2 minutes, being careful that it doesn't burn.

2. Add the peas (thawed and drained, if you're using frozen) and stir-fry for about 3 minutes. Stir in the ham, beans, tomatoes, broth, salt and pepper, and simmer for 5 minutes.

3. Toss the stir-fried bean mixture with the pasta and Parmesan cheese. (The ham in this dish makes it high in sodium, so consult your dietitian before including it in your menu plan if you are on a salt-restricted diet.)

### NUTRITIONAL ANALYSIS
(per serving):

Calories: 402
Protein: 20 g
Carbohydrate: 60 g
Fat: 9 g
Sat. Fat: 2 g
Cholesterol: 16 mg
Sodium: 659 mg
Fiber: 7 g
Exchange Approx.:
3 Lean Meats, ½ Vegetable, 2 Carbs./ Starches, 1 Fat

# Macaroni Casserole

1. Preheat oven to 350°F. Fry the ground turkey in a nonstick skillet; drain off any fat and pat the meat with paper towels. Add the onion and sauté with the ground turkey until transparent. Add the tomato paste and sauté until it starts to brown. Stir in the parsley, cinnamon, and salt and pepper, if using. Remove from heat and set aside.

2. Pour the milk in a bowl, add the potato flour, and whisk to mix. Stir in the macaroni and cheese.

3. Treat a 13" × 17" baking dish with nonstick spray. Pour half of the macaroni mixture into the pan. Spread the meat mixture over the macaroni. Add the rest of the macaroni, and top with the Béchamel Sauce. Bake for 1 hour.

## Little Bits

Don't waste the unused tomato paste left in the can. Spoon out tablespoon-sized portions and place them on plastic wrap or in sandwich baggies. Seal the packages and store in the freezer. When you need tomato paste in a recipe, add the frozen paste directly to sauce; there is no need to defrost.

**Serves 4**

½ pound (8 ounces) ground turkey
1 cup chopped onion
⅛ cup (2 tablespoons) unsalted tomato paste
1 teaspoon dried parsley
¼ teaspoon cinnamon
Kosher or sea salt and black pepper to taste (optional)
1 cup skim milk
1 tablespoon Ener-G potato flour
2 cups cooked macaroni
4 ounces Cabot's 50 percent Light Cheddar Cheese, grated (to yield 1 cup)
1 recipe Mock Béchamel Sauce (see page 24)

**NUTRITIONAL ANALYSIS**
(per serving, without salt):

Calories: 366
Protein: 29 g
Carbohydrate: 37 g
Fat: 12 g
Sat. Fat: 5 g
Cholesterol: 112 mg
Sodium: 324 mg
Fiber: 2
Exchange Approx.:
3 Very Lean Meats,
1 Medium-Fat Meat,
1 Carb./Starch, 1 Skim Milk

# Bleu Cheese Pasta

**Serves 4**

2 teaspoons olive oil
1 clove garlic, minced
½ cup nonfat cottage cheese
2 ounces crumbled bleu
   cheese
Skim milk (optional)
2 cups cooked pasta
¼ cup freshly grated
   Parmesan cheese
Freshly ground black pepper
   (optional)

1. Heat the olive oil in a large nonstick skillet. Add the garlic and sauté for a minute. Lower the heat, stir in the cottage cheese, and bring it to serving temperature.

2. Add the bleu cheese and stir to combine; thin the sauce with a little skim milk, if necessary. Toss with the pasta and divide into 4 equal servings. Top each serving with a tablespoon of the Parmesan cheese and freshly ground black pepper, if desired.

**NUTRITIONAL ANALYSIS**
(per serving):

Calories: 212
Protein: 12 g
Carbohydrate: 21 g
Fat: 9 g
Sat. Fat: 4 g
Cholesterol: 17 mg
Sodium: 317 mg
Fiber: 1 g
Exchange Approx.:
½ High Fat Meat,
½ Very Lean Meat,
½ Lean Meat, 1 Carb./
Starch, ½ Fat

# Soups and Stews

## chapter eight

# Eggplant and Tomato Stew

**Serves 4**

2 eggplants, trimmed but left
    whole
2 teaspoons olive oil
1 medium-sized Spanish
    onion, chopped
1 teaspoon chopped garlic
2 cups cooked or canned
    unsalted tomatoes,
    chopped with liquid
Optional seasonings to taste:
1 teaspoon hot pepper sauce
Ketchup
Nonfat plain yogurt
Fresh parsley sprigs

---

**NUTRITIONAL ANALYSIS**

(per serving):

Calories: 135
Protein: 4 g
Carbohydrate: 26 g
Fat: 3 g
Sat. Fat: trace
Cholesterol: 0 mg
Sodium: 22 mg
Fiber: 9 g
Exchange Approx.:
½ Fat, 4 Vegetables

1. Preheat oven to 400°F. Roast the eggplants on a baking sheet until soft, about 45 minutes. Remove all the meat from the eggplants. In a large sauté pan, heat the oil, then sauté the onions and garlic.

2. Add the eggplant and all the other ingredients, except the yogurt and parsley. Remove from heat and transfer the mixture to a food processor; pulse until it becomes creamy. Serve at room temperature, garnished with a dollop of yogurt and parsley, if desired.

## Too Salty?

If a soup, sauce, or liquid is too salty, peel and place a raw potato in the pot. Use half of a potato for each quart of liquid. Simmer, and then discard the potato (which will have absorbed some of the salt).

# Lentil Soup with Herbs and Lemon

1. Drain and rinse the lentils. Add the lentils and broth to a pot over medium heat and bring to a boil. Reduce the heat and simmer until tender, approximately 15 minutes. (If you did not pre-soak the lentils, increase the cooking time by about 15 more minutes.)

2. While the lentils are cooking, sauté the carrot, celery, and onion in oil for 8 minutes, or until the onion is golden brown. Remove from heat and set aside.

3. When the lentils are tender, add the vegetables, herbs, and salt and pepper, if using; cook for 2 minutes. Stir in the lemon juice and ladle into 4 serving bowls; garnish with lemon slices.

## Believe It or Not!

Put a fork at the bottom of the pan when you cook a pot of beans. The beans will cook in half the time.

**Serves 4**

1 cup lentils, soaked overnight in 1 cup water
6 cups low-fat, reduced-sodium chicken broth
1 carrot, sliced
1 stalk celery, sliced
1 yellow onion, thinly sliced
2 teaspoons olive oil
1 tablespoon dried tarragon
½ teaspoon dried oregano
Sea salt and black pepper to taste (optional)
1 tablespoon lemon juice
4 thin slices of lemon

**NUTRITIONAL ANALYSIS**
(per serving):

Calories: 214
Protein: 15 g
Carbohydrate: 34 g
Fat: 3 g
Sat. Fat: trace
Cholesterol: trace
Sodium: 353 mg
Fiber: 16 g
Exchange Approx.:
1 Lean Meat, 2
Starches, 1 Vegetable

# Lentil-Vegetable Soup

**Serves 4**

5 cups water or your choice
  of broth
1 medium-sized sweet potato,
  peeled and chopped
1 cup uncooked lentils
2 medium onions, chopped
¼ cup barley
2 tablespoons parsley flakes
2 carrots, sliced
1 celery stalk, chopped
2 teaspoons cumin

---

**NUTRITIONAL ANALYSIS**
(per serving, with water):

Calories: 273
Protein: 16 g
Carbohydrate: 53 g
Fat: 1 g
Sat. Fat: trace
Cholesterol: 0 mg
Sodium: 34 mg
Fiber: 19 g
Exchange Approx.:
1 Very Lean Meat, 3
Starches, 1 Vegetable

Combine all the ingredients in a soup pot and simmer until the lentils are soft, about 1 hour.

## Quick Lobster Bisque

A combination of lobster broth, tomato paste, and seasonings, Minor's Lobster Base makes this "soup" a rich and satisfying soup course or snack. Microwave ½ cup water and 1 teaspoon lobster base for 1 minute on high. Stir until the base is dissolved. Add in ½ cup milk. If the soup cools too much, microwave at 70 percent power for another 15 to 30 seconds. Nutritional Analysis (per cup): 57 calories if it's made with skim milk; 68 calories if you use Mock Cream (see page 20). Allow ½ Skim Milk and 1 Free exchange for either version.

# Tomato-Vegetable Soup

1. Heat the olive oil in a large stockpot and sauté the garlic, cumin, carrot, and celery for 1 minute; add the onion and cook until transparent. Stir in the tomato paste and sauté until it begins to brown.

2. Add the remaining ingredients except for the lime juice (or vinegar). Bring to a boil, then reduce heat and simmer for 20 to 30 minutes, adding additional broth or water, if needed. Just before serving, add the lime juice or balsamic vinegar.

*TIP: It isn't necessary to follow the sauté suggestions at the beginning of this recipe, but the soup will taste much richer if you do. (Sodium content will vary depending upon the broths used.)*

## Easy Measures

Consider freezing broth in an ice cube tray. Most ice cube tray sections hold ⅛ cup (2 tablespoons) of liquid. Once the broth is frozen, you can transfer the "cubes" to a freezer bag or container. This makes it easy to "measure" out the amount you'll need for recipes.

**Serves 6**

1 tablespoon olive oil
2 teaspoons minced garlic
⅔ teaspoon cumin
2 carrots, chopped
2 stalks celery, diced
1 medium onion, chopped
⅔ cup unsalted tomato paste
½ teaspoon red pepper flakes
2 cups canned, unsalted peeled tomatoes, with juice
⅔ teaspoon chopped fresh oregano
3 cups low-fat, reduced-sodium chicken broth
3 cups fat-free beef broth
2 cups diced potatoes
2 cups shredded cabbage
½ cup green beans
½ cup fresh or frozen corn kernels
½ teaspoon freshly cracked black pepper
¼ cup lime juice or balsamic vinegar

**NUTRITIONAL ANALYSIS**
(per serving):

Calories: 158
Protein: 5 g
Carbohydrate: 31 g
Fat: 3 g
Sat. Fat: trace
Cholesterol: trace
Sodium: 349 mg
Fiber: 5 g
Exchange Approx.:
1½ Starches/Vegetables, 1 Vegetable

# Baked Beef Stew

**Serves 4**

1 (12-ounce) can unsalted
   tomatoes, undrained
1 cup water
3 tablespoons quick-cooking
   tapioca
1 teaspoon Splenda granular
1 pound lean beef stew meat,
   trimmed of all fat, cut into
   1-inch pieces
4 medium carrots, cut into
   1-inch chunks
4 small potatoes, peeled and
   quartered
4 celery stalks, cut into ¾-
   inch chunks
2 medium onions, chopped
2 slices whole-wheat bread,
   torn into cubes

---

**NUTRITIONAL ANALYSIS**
(per serving):

Calories: 422
Protein: 30 g
Carbohydrate: 52 g
Fat: 11 g
Sat. Fat: 4 g
Cholesterol: 63 mg
Sodium: 331 mg
Fiber: 7 g
Exchange Approx.:
4 Lean Meats, 1
Starch/Vegetable,
1 Carb./Starch, 1 Veg-
etable

1. Preheat oven to 375°F. In a large bowl, combine the tomatoes, water, tapioca, and Splenda granular. Add all the remaining ingredients and mix well. Pour into a baking dish treated with nonstick spray.

2. Cover and bake for 2 hours or until the meat and vegetables are tender.

## Flavor Saver

If you discover that you've scorched a soup, don't stir it or scrape the bottom. Stirring is what distributes the burned flavor. Carefully pour the liquid into another pan. You should be able to salvage what remains. (If it still tastes slightly burnt, adding a little milk should remove that disagreeable flavor. For acidic soups, add some grape jelly.)

# Cold Roasted Red Pepper Soup

1. Heat a saucepan over medium-high heat. Add the olive oil and sauté the onion until transparent. Add the peppers and broth. Bring to a boil, then reduce the heat and simmer for 15 minutes. Remove from heat and purée in a blender or food processor until smooth.

2. Allow the soup to cool, then stir in the yogurt and the salt, if using; chill well in the refrigerator. Garnish the soup with fresh basil sprigs, if desired.

**Serves 4**

1 teaspoon olive oil
½ cup chopped onion
3 roasted red bell peppers, seeded and chopped
3¼ cups low-fat, reduced-sodium chicken broth
½ cup nonfat plain yogurt
½ teaspoon sea salt (optional)
4 sprigs fresh basil (optional)

**NUTRITIONAL ANALYSIS**
(per serving, without salt):

Calories: 73
Protein: 5 g
Carbohydrate: 9 g
Fat: 4 g
Sat. Fat: 1 g
Cholesterol: 3 mg
Sodium: 404 mg
Fiber: 3 g
Exchange Approx.:
½ Fat, ½ Starch

# Nutty Greek Snapper Soup

**Serves 4**

1-pound (16-ounce) red
    snapper fillet
2 large cucumbers
4 green onions, chopped
3 tablespoons lime juice
4 cups nonfat plain yogurt
¼ cup chopped walnuts
1 cup, packed, mixed fresh
    parsley, basil, cilantro,
    arugula, and chives
Salt and pepper to taste
    (optional)
Herb sprigs, for garnish
    (optional)

---

**NUTRITIONAL ANALYSIS**
(per serving):

Calories: 309
Protein: 39 g
Carbohydrate: 25 g
Fat: 6 g
Sat. Fat: trace
Cholesterol: 46 mg
Sodium: 240 mg
Fiber: 2 g
Exchange Approx.:
4 Lean Meats, 1 Skim
Milk, 1 Vegetable

1. Rinse the red snapper fillet and pat dry with paper towels. Broil the fillet until opaque through the thickest part, about 4 minutes on each side, depending on the thickness of the fillet. Let cool. (Alternatives would be to steam or poach the fillets.)

2. Peel and halve the cucumbers, then scoop out and discard the seeds; cut into roughly 1-inch pieces. Put half the cucumber with the green onions in the bowl of a food processor. Use the pulse button to coarsely chop; transfer to a large bowl. Add the remaining cucumber, yogurt, and herb leaves to the food processor and process until smooth and frothy. (Alternatively, you can grate the cucumbers, finely mince the green onion and herbs, and then stir them together with the yogurt in a large bowl.) Stir the lime juice into the soup and season with salt and pepper to taste, if using. Cover and refrigerate for at least 1 hour, or up to 8 hours; the longer the soup cools, the more the flavors will mellow.

3. While the soup cools, break the cooled red snapper fillet into large chunks, discarding the skin and any bones. Ladle the chilled soup into shallow bowls and add the red snapper. Sprinkle the chopped walnuts over the soup, garnish with herb sprigs, and serve.

*TIP: You can make this soup using leftover fish, or substitute halibut, cod, or sea bass for the snapper.*

# Vegetable and Bean Chili

1. Heat a heavy pot over moderately high heat. Add the olive oil, onions, bell pepper, garlic, and jalapeño; sauté until the vegetables are softened, about 5 minutes. Add the chili powder and cumin, and sauté for 1 minute, stirring frequently to mix well.

2. Chop the tomatoes and add them, with their juice, and the zucchini. Bring to a boil; lower heat and simmer, partially covered, for 15 minutes, stirring occasionally. Stir in the beans and chocolate and simmer, stirring occasionally, for an additional 5 minutes, or until the beans are heated through and the chocolate is melted. Stir in the cilantro, and serve.

**Serves 8**

4 teaspoons olive oil
2 cups chopped cooking onions
½ cup chopped green bell pepper
3 cloves garlic, chopped
1 small jalapeño pepper, finely chopped (Only include the seeds if you like the chili extra hot!)
1 tablespoon chili powder
1 teaspoon ground cumin
1 (28-ounce) can unsalted tomatoes, undrained
2 zucchini, peeled and chopped
2 (15-ounce) cans unsalted kidney beans, rinsed
1 tablespoon chopped sugar-free dark chocolate
3 tablespoons chopped fresh cilantro

**NUTRITIONAL ANALYSIS**
(per serving):

Calories: 164
Protein: 8 g
Carbohydrate: 28 g
Fat: 4 g
Sat. Fat: 1 g
Cholesterol: 28 mg
Sodium: 531 mg
Fiber: 7 g
Exchange Approx.: 1 Lean Meat, 2 Starches, 1 Vegetable

# Rich and Creamy Sausage-Potato Soup

**Serves 2**

1 teaspoon olive oil
½ teaspoon butter
½ cup chopped onion,
    steamed
1 clove roasted garlic
1 ounce crumbled, cooked
    Chorizo (see page 97)
¼ teaspoon celery seed
2 Yukon gold potatoes, peeled
    and diced into 1-inch pieces
½ cup fat-free chicken broth
1½ cup Mock Cream (see
    page 20)
1 teaspoon white wine vinegar
1 teaspoon vanilla extract*
Optional seasonings to taste:
Fresh parsley

*Vanilla extract contains a
trace amount of sugar.
You can substitute sugar-
free organic extract if you
prefer.*

1. In a saucepan, heat the olive oil and butter over medium heat. Add the onion, roasted garlic, chorizo, celery seed, and potatoes; sauté until the mixture is heated. Add the chicken broth and bring the mixture to a boil.

2. Cover the saucepan, reduce heat, and maintain simmer for 10 minutes, or until the potatoes are tender. Add the Mock Cream and heat. Remove pan from the burner and stir in the vinegar and vanilla.

## Skim the Fat

You can remove fat from soups and stews by dropping ice cubes into the pot. The fat will cling to the cubes as you stir. Be sure to take out the cubes before they melt. Fat also clings to lettuce leaves; simply sweep them over the top of the soup. Discard ice cubes or leaves when you're done.

---

**NUTRITIONAL ANALYSIS**
(per serving):

Calories: 326
Protein: 17 g
Carbohydrate: 53 g
Fat: 6 g
Sat. Fat: 2 g
Cholesterol: 19 mg
Sodium: 259 mg
Fiber: 3 g
Exchange Approx.:
1 Fat, ½ Medium-Fat
Meat, 1 Starchy Vege-
table, 1½ Skim Milks,
1 Vegetable

# Chicken Corn Chowder

1. Spray a large soup pot with nonstick cooking spray and heat on medium setting until hot. Add the chicken, onion, and bell pepper; sauté over medium heat until the chicken is browned and the vegetables are tender. Stir in the potatoes and broth, and bring to a boil. Reduce the heat and simmer, covered, for 20 minutes. Stir in the corn.

2. Blend the flour and milk in a bowl, then gradually stir it into the pot. Increase heat to medium and cook until the mixture comes to a boil, then reduce heat and simmer until soup is thickened, stirring constantly. Add the cheese and stir until it's melted and blended into the soup. Add the salt and pepper to taste, and sprinkle with bacon bits before serving.

*TIP: To trim down the fat in this recipe, use a reduced fat cheese, such as Cabot's 50 percent Light Cheddar.*

**Serves 10**

1 pound boneless, skinless chicken breast, cut into chunks
1 medium onion, chopped
1 red bell pepper, diced
1 large potato, diced
2 (16-ounce) cans low-fat, reduced-sodium chicken broth
1 (8¾-ounce) can unsalted cream-style corn
½ cup all-purpose flour
2 cups skim milk
4 ounces Cheddar cheese, diced
½ teaspoon sea salt
Freshly ground pepper to taste
½ cup processed bacon bits

**NUTRITIONAL ANALYSIS**
(per serving):

Calories: 193
Protein: 17 g
Carbohydrate: 21 g
Fat: 5 g
Sat. Fat: 3 g
Cholesterol: 39 mg
Sodium: 155 mg
Fiber: 2 g
Exchange Approx.:
1½ Very Lean Meats,
½ Starchy Vegetable,
1 Vegetable, ½ Skim
Milk, ½ High-Fat Meat

# Smoked Mussel Chowder

**Serves 6**

2 tablespoons olive oil
1 medium onion, chopped
2 carrots, diced
2 stalks celery, diced
½ bulb fennel, diced
1 teaspoon chopped garlic
4 red potatoes, cut into ½-inch cubes
1 cup dry white wine
2½ cups clam juice
1 bay leaf
Pinch of cayenne pepper
½ teaspoon thyme
2 medium-sized white potatoes, peeled and quartered (to yield 2½ cups)
1 cup skim milk
4 ounces Ducktrap River smoked mussels
Sea salt and freshly ground black pepper to taste (optional)
Fresh parsley sprigs (optional)

1. Heat the olive oil in soup pot. Add the onions, carrots, celery, fennel, and garlic; gently sauté for 10 minutes. (Do not brown vegetables.) Add the red potatoes, wine, clam juice, bay leaf, cayenne and thyme. Let the soup simmer until the potatoes are cooked.

2. In a separate pan of boiling water, cook the white potatoes until tender. Mash the potatoes by putting them through a potato ricer or into the bowl of a food processor along with some of the skim milk. Once the red potatoes in the chowder are tender, stir in the mashed potatoes, remaining milk, and mussels. Do not let the soup come to a boil. Salt and pepper to taste and serve garnished with parsley sprigs, if desired.

**NUTRITIONAL ANALYSIS**
(per serving):

Calories: 273
Protein: 8 g
Carbohydrate: 37 g
Fat: 8 g
Sat. Fat: 2 g
Cholesterol: 21 mg
Sodium: 579 mg
Fiber: 3 g
Exchange Approx.:
1 Fat, 1 Lean Meat,
2 Vegetables/Starches,
1 Vegetable

# Salmon Chowder

1. Drain and flake the salmon, discarding liquid. In large nonstick saucepan, melt the butter over medium heat; sauté the onion, celery, green pepper, garlic, and carrots, stirring often until the vegetables are tender, about 5 minutes.

2. Add the potatoes, broth, water, pepper, and dill seed; bring to boil. Reduce heat, cover, and simmer for 20 minutes, or until the potatoes are tender. Add the zucchini; simmer, covered, for another 5 minutes.

3. Add the salmon, Mock Cream, corn, and pepper. Cook over low heat just until heated through. Just before serving, add parsley, if desired.

**Serves 4**

1 (7½-ounce) can unsalted salmon
2 teaspoons butter
1 medium onion, chopped
2 stalks celery, chopped
1 sweet green pepper, seeded and chopped
1 clove garlic, minced
4 carrots, peeled and diced
4 small potatoes, peeled and diced
1 cup fat-free chicken broth
1 cup water
½ teaspoon cracked black pepper
½ teaspoon dill seed
1 cup diced zucchini
1 cup Mock Cream (page 20)
1 (8¾-ounce) can unsalted cream-style corn
Freshly ground black pepper to taste
½ cup chopped fresh parsley (optional)

---

**NUTRITIONAL ANALYSIS**
(per serving):

Calories: 364
Protein: 20 g
Carbohydrate: 61 g
Fat: 6 g
Sat. Fat: 2 g
Cholesterol: 28 mg
Sodium: 199 mg
Fiber: 7 g
Exchange Approx.: ½ Fat, 2 Starches/Vegetables, 2 Lean Meats, 2 Vegetables, ½ Skim Milk

Vegetable Broth

Layered Veggie Casserole

Creamy Polenta

Healthy Onion Rings

Oven-Baked Red Potatoes

Baked French Fries

Baked Potato Chips

Sweet Potato Crisps

Fluffy Buttermilk Mashed Potatoes

Roasted Garlic Mashed Potatoes

Corn Casserole

Gnocchi

# Veggies and Sides

## chapter nine

# Vegetable Broth

**Yields about 2½ quarts**
**Serving size: ¾ cup**

4 carrots, peeled and chopped
2 celery stalks and leaves, chopped
1 green bell pepper, seeded and chopped
2 medium zucchini, chopped
1 small onion, chopped
1 cup chopped fresh spinach
2 cups chopped leeks
½ cup chopped scallions
1 cup chopped green beans
1 cup chopped parsnips
2 bay leaves
2 cloves garlic, crushed
Sea salt and freshly ground black pepper (optional)
3 quarts water

**NUTRITIONAL ANALYSIS**
(per serving):

Calories: 10
Protein: trace
Carbohydrate: 2 g
Fat: trace
Sat. Fat: trace
Cholesterol: 0 mg
Sodium: 8 mg
Fiber: 1 g
Exchange Approx.:
1 Free Vegetable

1. Place all of the ingredients in a large pot and bring to a boil. Reduce the heat, cover the pan, and simmer for 30 minutes, or until vegetables are tender. Discard the bay leaf. Use a slotted spoon to transfer the vegetables to a different pot and mix them with some of the broth for "Free Exchange" vegetable soup. Freeze this mixture in single-serving containers to keep on hand for a quick, heat-in-the-microwave snack.

2. Strain the remaining vegetables from the broth, purée them in a blender or food processor, and return to the broth to add dietary fiber and add some body to the broth. Cool and freeze the broth until needed.

*TIP: If you strain the vegetables and discard them, a ½-cup serving size of the broth will have approximately 5 calories, and will still count as 1 Free Vegetable.*

## Perpetual Broth

The easiest way to create vegetable broth is to keep a container in your freezer for saving the liquid from cooked vegetables. Vegetable broth makes a great addition to sauces, soups, and many other recipes. You can substitute it for meat broth in most recipes or use it instead of water for cooking pasta, rice, or other grains.

# Layered Veggie Casserole

1. Preheat oven to 350°F. Using a large casserole dish treated with nonstick spray, layer the frozen mixed vegetables, onion, and pepper. Mix the tomato juice with the seasonings and 2 tablespoons of the Parmesan cheese, and pour it over the vegetables. Cover and bake for 1 hour.

2. Uncover, sprinkle with remaining Parmesan cheese, and continue to bake for 10 minutes, or until the liquid thickens and the mixture bubbles.

## Season First

When you ready vegetables for steaming them, add fresh or dried herbs, spices, sliced or diced onions, minced garlic, grated ginger, or just about any other seasoning you'd normally use. The seasonings will cook into the vegetables during steaming.

**Serves 4**

1 (10-ounce) package frozen
     mixed vegetables
½ cup diced onion
½ cup diced green pepper
1 cup unsalted tomato juice
⅛ teaspoon celery seed
⅛ teaspoon dried basil
⅛ teaspoon dried oregano
⅛ teaspoon dried parsley
¼ teaspoon garlic powder
3 tablespoons grated
     Parmesan cheese, divided

**NUTRITIONAL ANALYSIS**
(per serving):

Calories: 84
Protein: 5 g
Carbohydrate: 16 g
Fat: 1 g
Sat. Fat: 1 g
Cholesterol: 3 mg
Sodium: 101 mg
Fiber: 4 g
Exchange Approx.:
1 Vegetable, 1 Starch/
Vegetable

# Creamy Polenta

**Serves 4**

1 cup skim milk
½ cup nonfat cottage cheese
¼ cup yellow cornmeal

**NUTRITIONAL ANALYSIS**
(per serving):

Calories: 64
Protein: 6 g
Carbohydrate: 9 g
Fat: trace
Sat. Fat: trace
Cholesterol: 2 mg
Sodium: 37 mg
Fiber: 1 g
Exchange Approx.:
½ Starch, ½ Skim Milk

1. Add the milk and cottage cheese to a blender and process until smooth. Pour the mixture into a nonstick, heavy saucepan.

2. Over medium heat and stirring occasionally to prevent it from scorching, heat it until it begins to steam. Slowly stir in the cornmeal. Cook, stirring constantly, for 15 minutes.

# Healthy Onion Rings

1. Preheat oven to 350°F. Dredge the onion slices in the flour, shaking off any excess. Dip the onions in yogurt, then dredge them through the bread crumbs.

2. Prepare a baking sheet with nonstick cooking spray. Arrange the onion rings on the pan, and bake for 15 to 20 minutes. Place the onion rings under the broiler for an additional 2 minutes to brown them. Season with salt and pepper, if desired.

**Serves 4**

1 cup yellow onion slices (¼-inch thick)
½ cup flour
½ cup nonfat plain yogurt
½ cup bread crumbs
Sea salt and freshly ground black pepper to taste (optional)

**NUTRITIONAL ANALYSIS**
(per serving, without salt):

Calories: 111
Protein: 4 g
Carbohydrate: 22 g
Fat: 1 g
Sat. Fat: trace
Cholesterol: 1 mg
Sodium: 255 mg
Fiber: 1 g
Exchange Approx.:
1 Vegetable, 1 Carb./Starch

# Oven-Baked Red Potatoes

**Serves 4**

1 pound (16 ounces) small red
    potatoes, halved
¼ cup fresh lemon juice
1 teaspoon olive oil
1 teaspoon sea salt
¼ teaspoon freshly ground
    pepper

---

**NUTRITIONAL ANALYSIS**
(per serving):

Calories: 120
Protein: 2 g
Carbohydrate: 26 g
Fat: 1 g
Sat. Fat: trace
Cholesterol: 0 g
Sodium: 587 mg
Fiber: 2 g
Exchange Approx.:
1 Starch/Vegetable

1. Preheat oven to 350°F. Arrange the potatoes in a 13" × 9" ovenproof casserole dish. Combine the remaining ingredients, and pour over the potatoes.

2. Bake for 30 to 40 minutes, or until the potatoes are tender, turning 3 to 4 times to baste.

## Remember the Roasting "Rack"

Use caution when roasting potatoes with meat. The potatoes will act like a sponge and soak up the fat. Your best option, of course, is to use lean cuts of meat and elevate the meat and vegetables out of the fat by putting them on a roasting rack within the pan. Or, make a "bridge" by elevating the meat on stalks of celery. Discard the celery that you've used to elevate the meat.

# Baked French Fries

1. Preheat oven to 400°F. Wash, peel, and slice the potatoes into French fry wedges. Wrap the slices in a paper towel to remove any excess moisture. "Oil" the potatoes by placing them into a plastic bag with the olive oil. Close the bag and shake the potatoes until they're evenly coated. Spread potatoes on a baking sheet treated with nonstick spray and bake for 5 to 10 minutes.

2. Remove the pan from the oven and quickly turn the potatoes. Return the pan to the oven and bake for another 10 to 15 minutes, depending on how crisp you prefer your fries. Season the potatoes with salt and pepper, if your diet allows for the additional sodium.

## Get a Head Start

Speed up the time it takes to bake French fries! First, cook the potatoes in the microwave for 3 to 4 minutes in a covered microwave-safe dish. Allow potatoes to rest for at least a minute after removing the dish from the microwave. Dry potatoes with paper towels, if necessary. Arrange the potatoes on a nonstick spray–treated baking sheet. Spray the potatoes with flavored cooking spray or a few spritzes of olive oil and bake at 400°F for 5 to 8 minutes to crisp them.

**Serves 1**

1 small white potato (3 ounces)
1 teaspoon olive oil
Sea salt and freshly ground black pepper to taste (optional)

**NUTRITIONAL ANALYSIS**
(per serving, without salt):

Calories: 119
Protein: 2 g
Carbohydrate: 18 g
Fat: 5 g
Sat. Fat: 1 g
Cholesterol: 0 mg
Sodium: 4 mg
Fiber: 1 g
Exchange Approx.:
1 Starch, 1 Fat

# Baked Potato Chips

**Serves 1**

1 small white potato (3
ounces)
1 teaspoon olive oil
Sea salt and freshly ground
black pepper to taste
(optional)

---

**NUTRITIONAL ANALYSIS**
(per serving, without salt):

Calories: 119
Protein: 2 g
Carbohydrate: 18 g
Fat: 5 g
Sat. Fat: 1 g
Cholesterol: 0 mg
Sodium: 4 mg
Fiber: 1 g
Exchange Approx.:
1 Starch, 1 Fat

1. Preheat oven to 400°F. Wash, peel, and thinly slice the potatoes. Wrap the slices in a paper towel to remove any excess moisture. Spread the potatoes on a baking sheet treated with nonstick spray and spritz them with olive oil.

2. Bake for 10 to 15 minutes, depending on how crisp you prefer your chips. Season the potatoes with salt and pepper, if your diet allows for the additional sodium.

*TIP: The Nutritional Allowance for this recipe allows for the teaspoon of olive oil. Even though you just spritz the potatoes with oil, remember that "chips" have more surface area than fries do.*

## Fat-Cutting Alternatives

Eliminate the oil (and thus the Fat Exchange) in the Baked French Fries and Baked Potato Chips in this chapter by using butter-flavored or olive oil cooking spray instead.

# Sweet Potato Crisps

1. Preheat oven to 400°F. Scrub the sweet potato or yam and pierce the flesh several times with a fork. Place on a microwave-safe plate and microwave for 5 minutes on high. Remove from the microwave and wrap the sweet potato in aluminum foil. Set aside for 5 minutes.

2. Remove the foil, peel the potato, and cut it into "French fries." Spread the fries on a baking sheet treated with nonstick spray and spritz with the olive oil. Bake for 10 to 15 minutes, or until crisp. There's a risk that sweet potato strips (French fries) will caramelize and burn. Check them often while cooking to ensure this doesn't occur; lower the oven temperature, if necessary. Season with salt and pepper, if desired.

**Serves 2**

1 small sweet potato or yam
1 teaspoon olive oil
Sea salt and freshly ground
    black pepper to taste
    (optional)

**NUTRITIONAL ANALYSIS**
(per serving, without salt):

Calories: 89
Protein: 1 g
Carbohydrate: 16 g
Fat: 2 g
Sat. Fat: trace
Cholesterol: 0 mg
Sodium: 7 mg
Fiber: 9 g
Exchange Approx.:
1 Starch, ½ Fat

# Fluffy Buttermilk Mashed Potatoes

**Serves 4**

¾ pound (12 ounces) peeled,
   boiled potatoes
¼ cup warm buttermilk
2 teaspoons unsalted butter
Sea salt and freshly ground
   black pepper to taste
   (optional)

**NUTRITIONAL ANALYSIS**
(per serving, without salt):

Calories: 97
Protein: 2 g
Carbohydrate: 18 g
Fat: 2 g
Sat. Fat: 1 g
Cholesterol: 6 mg
Sodium: 20 mg
Fiber: 2 g
Exchange Approx.:
1 Starch, ½ Fat

1. Place the potatoes in a large bowl and partially mash. Add the warm buttermilk and mix well, mashing the potatoes completely.

2. Stir in the butter and salt and pepper (if using). (If you like your mashed potatoes creamy, add some of the potato water.)

# Roasted Garlic Mashed Potatoes

Combine all the ingredients and whip until fluffy. If the potatoes or cauliflower are overly moist, add the buttermilk gradually until the whipped mixture reaches the desired consistency. (Combining steamed cauliflower with the potatoes allows you to increase the portion size without significantly changing the flavor of the mashed potatoes.)

## Gravy Substitute

Instead of using gravy, sprinkle crumbled bleu cheese or grated Parmesan over mashed potatoes. Just remember that cheese is a Meat Exchange and adjust the Exchange Approximations for each serving accordingly.

**Serves 4**

4 cloves roasted garlic
1 small onion, chopped
¾ pound (12 ounces) peeled, cooked potatoes
2 cups cauliflower, steamed and drained
¼ cup buttermilk
⅛ cup nonfat cottage cheese
2 teaspoons unsalted butter
Sea salt and freshly ground black pepper to taste (optional)

**NUTRITIONAL ANALYSIS**
(per serving, without salt):

Calories: 126
Protein: 4 g
Carbohydrate: 23 g
Fat: 2 g
Sat. Fat: 1 g
Cholesterol: 6 mg
Sodium: 31 mg
Fiber: 3 g
Exchange Approx.:
1 Starch, 1 Vegetable, ½ Fat

# Corn Casserole

**Serves 2**

1 tablespoon finely chopped
onion
1 tablespoon finely chopped
green or red bell pepper
1 cup frozen or fresh corn
kernels
⅛ teaspoon ground mace
Dash ground white or black
pepper
¾ cup skim milk
¼ cup nonfat dry milk
1 egg
1 teaspoon butter

**NUTRITIONAL ANALYSIS**
(per serving):

Calories: 188
Protein: 11 g
Carbohydrate: 32 g
Fat: 3 g
Sat. Fat: 1 g
Cholesterol: 10 mg
Sodium: 133 mg
Fiber: 2 g
Exchange Approx.:
1½ Starches, 1 Skim
Milk, ½ Fat

1. Preheat oven to 325°F. In a medium-sized bowl, combine the onion, bell pepper, corn, mace, and pepper, and toss to mix.

2. In a blender, combine the skim milk, dry milk, egg, and butter, and process until mixed. Pour over the corn mixture and toss to mix. Pour the entire mixture into a glass casserole dish treated with nonstick spray. Bake for 1 hour, or until set.

## Special Spice Side Effects

Ground mace or nutmeg can elevate blood pressure or cause an irregular heartbeat in some individuals. Check with your doctor or nutritionist before you add it to your diet.

# Gnocchi

1. Combine the potato, flour, and egg in a large bowl. Knead until the dough forms a ball. The finished dough should be smooth, pliable, and slightly sticky. Shape 4 equal portions of the dough into long ropes, about ¾ inch in diameter. On a floured surface, cut the rope into ½-inch pieces. Press your thumb or forefinger into each piece to create an indentation. (Some gnocchi chefs also like to roll each piece with a fork to add a distinctive texture.)

2. Bring a large pot of water to a boil. Drop in the gnocchi, being careful that the amount you add doesn't stop the water from boiling. Cook for 3 to 5 minutes, or until the gnocchi rise to the top. Remove the gnocchi from water with a slotted spoon. Serve immediately, or, if you make it in batches, put finished gnocchi on a platter to be set in a warm oven.

*TIP: As a side dish, serve gnocchi with your favorite pasta sauce or dress it with a little olive oil and herbs or Parmesan cheese. (Be sure to add the extra Exchange Approximations if you do.)*

## Old Country Secrets

Italian cooks sometimes toss each helping of gnocchi in a teaspoon of melted butter and Splenda granular, then sprinkle it with cinnamon to serve it as a dessert. This adds 1 Fat Exchange and 1 Carb exchange to the Gnocchi recipe.

**Serves 8**

1 cup boiled, mashed potatoes
1 egg
2 cups all-purpose or semolina flour

**NUTRITIONAL ANALYSIS**
(per serving):

Calories: 139
Protein: 4 g
Carbohydrate: 28 g
Fat: 1 g
Sat. Fat: trace
Cholesterol: 23 mg
Sodium: 9 mg
Fiber: 1 g
PCF Ratio: 12-82-6
Exchange Approx.:
1½ Starches

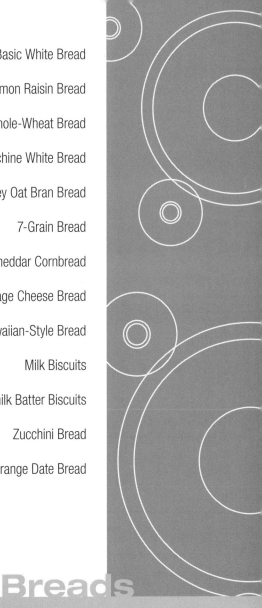

# Breads

chapter ten

# Basic White Bread

**Yields 2 large loaves
(40 slices)
Serving size: 1 slice**

5½–6 cups flour
1 package (2½ teaspoons)
   active dry yeast
¼ cup warm water
2 tablespoons Splenda
   granular
1¾ cups warm potato water or
   plain water
2 tablespoons shortening
1 tablespoon sea salt

**NUTRITIONAL ANALYSIS**
(per serving):

Calories: 75
Protein: 2 g
Carbohydrate: 14 g
Fat: 1 g
Sat. Fat: trace
Cholesterol: 0 mg
Sodium: 142 mg
Fiber: 1 g
Exchange Approx.:
1 Bread/Starch

1. Place about a third of the flour in a large bowl and set aside. Mix the yeast with the ¼ cup warm water in another bowl, stirring well. Add the Splenda granular and potato water to the yeast; add that mixture to the flour in the bowl and stir well. Set aside for 5 minutes to allow the yeast to "proof."

2. Stir the mixture and cut in the shortening using a pastry blender or your hands. Stir in the salt and as much of the remaining flour as possible. The dough has enough flour when it's still somewhat sticky to the touch, yet pulls away from the side of the bowl as it's stirred. Turn the dough onto a lightly floured work surface. Knead for 8 to 10 minutes until smooth and elastic, adding flour as necessary. The dough will take on an almost "glossy" appearance once it's been kneaded sufficiently.

3. Transfer the dough to a bowl treated with nonstick spray. Cover with a damp cloth and place in a warm, draft-free area. Allow to rise until double in volume, about 1 to 1½ hours.

4. Punch the dough down and let it rise a second time until almost doubled in bulk.

5. Treat two 9" × 5" bread pans with nonstick spray. Punch the dough down again and divide into 2 loaves. Shape the loaves and place in the prepared bread pans. Cover and let rise until almost doubled.

6. Preheat oven to 350°F. Bake for 20 to 30 minutes, or until golden brown. Remove bread from pans and allow to cool on a rack.

## Bread Basics

Always place bread pans and muffin tins in the center of the oven to allow proper heat circulation.

# Cinnamon Raisin Bread

1. Toss the raisins with 1 tablespoon of flour to coat them; shake off excess. When stirring in the bulk of the flour, add the raisins (Step 2 of Basic White Bread).

2. While following steps 3–4 for Basic White Bread, mix together ⅓ cup Splenda granular and 2½ teaspoons cinnamon in a separate bowl. Divide the dough in half (Step 5 of Basic White Bread). Using a rolling pin, roll each half into a rectangular shape about ½-inch thick. Use a pastry brush to brush each rectangle with enough water to dampen the dough. Divide the cinnamon-Splenda granular mixture into 2 equal portions. Sprinkle across the dampened surface of the dough.

3. Starting at a long end of the rectangle, use your fingers to roll the dough. Place it in a 9" x 5" loaf pan, tucking under the ends of the dough. Repeat with the second rectangle of dough. Allow to rise until doubled in bulk, and bake according to the instructions for Basic White Bread.

## Any Way You Slice It . . .

It's usually easier to slice a loaf of homemade bread into 10 thicker slices than into 20 thinner ones. To arrive at 1 serving, either cut each thick slice in half or remove the crusts. (Be sure to reserve the crusts for use in other recipes.)

**Yields 2 large loaves (40 slices)**
**Serving size: 1 slice**

Basic White Bread recipe
1 cup raisins

---

**NUTRITIONAL ANALYSIS**
(per serving):

Calories: 95
Protein: 2 g
Carbohydrate: 20 g
Fat: 1 g
Sat. Fat: trace
Cholesterol: 0 mg
Sodium: 175 mg
Fiber: 1 g
Exchange Approx.:
1 Bread/Starch; ½ Fruit

# Whole-Wheat Bread

**Yields 2 loaves (40 slices)**
**Serving size: 1 slice**

1 package (2½ teaspoons) active dry yeast
2 cups warm water
3 cups unbleached all-purpose or bread flour
2 tablespoons Splenda granular
½ cup hot water
2 teaspoons salt
½ cup honey
3 tablespoons shortening
3 cups whole-wheat flour

---

**NUTRITIONAL ANALYSIS**
(per serving):

Calories: 90
Protein: 3 g
Carbohydrate: 18 g
Fat: 1 g
Sat. Fat: trace
Cholesterol: 0 mg
Sodium: 108 mg
Fiber: 1 g
Exchange Approx.:
1 Bread/Starch

1. Add the yeast to the 2 cups warm water. Stir in the all-purpose flour and Splenda granular. Beat the mixture until smooth, either by hand or with a mixer. Set the mixture in a warm place to "proof" until it becomes foamy and bubbly (up to 1 hour).

2. Combine the ½ cup hot water, the salt, honey, and shortening; stir. Allow to cool to lukewarm. (Stirring the Splenda granular until it's dissolved should be sufficient to cool the water; test to be sure, as adding liquid that's too warm can "kill" the yeast.) Add to the bubbly flour mixture (the "sponge"). Stir in the whole-wheat flour and beat until smooth, but do not knead.

3. Divide the dough into 2 lightly greased pans, cover, and set in a warm place until doubled in size. Preheat oven to 350°F and bake for 50 minutes.

## History Lesson

The sponge process of making bread was more popular years ago, when foodstuffs were less processed and the quality of yeast was less reliable. The yeast works in a batter and the dough rises only once. The sponge process produces a loaf that is lighter but coarser grained.

# Bread Machine
# White Bread

Add the ingredients to your bread machine in the order recommended by the manufacturer, being careful that the yeast doesn't come in contact with the salt.

**Yields 1 large loaf (24 slices)**
**Serving size: 1 slice**

1¼ cups skim milk
2 tablespoons nonfat milk powder
1 tablespoon olive or canola oil
1 teaspoon sea salt
1 tablespoon Splenda granular
4 cups unbleached all-purpose or bread flour
1 package (2½ teaspoons) active dry yeast

**NUTRITIONAL ANALYSIS**
(per serving):

Calories: 88
Protein: 3 g
Carbohydrate: 17 g
Fat: 1 g
Sat. Fat: trace
Cholesterol: trace
Sodium: 87 mg
Fiber: 1 g
Exchange Approx.:
1 Bread/Starch

# Honey Oat Bran Bread

**Yields 1 large loaf
(24 slices)
Serving size: 1 slice**

1¼ cups skim milk
2 tablespoons nonfat
  buttermilk powder
1 tablespoon olive or canola
  oil
1 medium egg
1 cup oat bran
1 teaspoon sea salt
½ cup whole-wheat flour
2½ cups unbleached all-
  purpose or bread flour
1 tablespoon honey
1 package (2½ teaspoons)
  active dry yeast

**NUTRITIONAL ANALYSIS**
(per serving):

Calories: 86
Protein: 3 g
Carbohydrate: 16 g
Fat: 1 g
Sat. Fat: trace
Cholesterol: 8 mg
Sodium: 109 mg
Fiber: 1 g
Exchange Approx.:
1 Bread/Starch

Use the light-crust setting on your bread machine, and add the ingredients to your bread machine in the order recommended by the manufacturer. Be careful that the yeast doesn't come in contact with the salt.

# 7-Grain Bread

Add the ingredients to your bread machine in the order recommended by the manufacturer, being careful that the yeast doesn't come in contact with the salt. Bake on whole-wheat bread setting.

## Lactose-Free Bread

When cooking for someone who is lactose intolerant, substitute equal amounts of water or soy milk for any milk called for in bread recipes.

**Yield: 1 large loaf (24 slices)**
**Serving size: 1 slice**

1¼ cups skim milk
2 tablespoons nonfat milk powder
1 tablespoon olive or canola oil
¾ cup dry 7-grain cereal
½ cup oat bran
1 teaspoon sea salt
2¼ cups unbleached all-purpose or bread flour
½ cup whole-wheat flour
1 tablespoon honey
1 package (2½ teaspoons) dry yeast

**NUTRITIONAL ANALYSIS**
(per serving):

Calories: 82
Protein: 3 g
Carbohydrate: 15 g
Fat: 1 g
Sat. Fat: trace
Cholesterol: 8 mg
Sodium: 108 mg
Fiber: 1 g
Exchange Approx.:
1 Bread/Starch

# Cheddar Cornbread

**Yields 1 large loaf**
**(24 slices)**
**Serving size: 1 slice**

1¼ cup water
1 tablespoon honey
3 tablespoons butter
¼ cup nonfat milk powder
1 package (2½ teaspoons)
   active dry yeast
2½ cups unbleached all-
   purpose or bread flour
1 cup yellow cornmeal
1½ teaspoons sea salt
⅔ cup grated Cheddar cheese

---

**NUTRITIONAL ANALYSIS**
(per serving):

Calories: 102
Protein: 3 g
Carbohydrate: 16 g
Fat: 3 g
Sat. Fat: 2 g
Cholesterol: 7 mg
Sodium: 172 mg
Fiber: 1 g
Exchange Approx.:
1 Bread/Starch, ½ Fat

Use the light-crust setting, and add all the ingredients except the cheese in the order suggested by your bread machine manual. Process on the basic bread cycle according to the manufacturer's directions. At the beeper (or at the end of the first kneading), add the cheese.

# Cottage Cheese Bread

Add the ingredients to your bread machine in the order recommended by the manufacturer, being careful that the yeast doesn't come in contact with the salt. Check the bread machine at the "beep" to make sure the dough is pulling away from the sides of the pan and forming a ball. Add water or flour, if needed. (Note: You do not want the dough to be overly dry.) Bake at the white bread setting, light crust.

## Why Breads Need Salt

Salt is only used in bread to enhance the flavor. If salt comes directly in contact with the yeast before the yeast has had a chance to begin to work, it can hinder the action of the yeast. Keep that in mind when you add ingredients to your bread machine.

**Yields 1 large loaf
(24 slices)
Serving size: 1 slice**

¼ cup water
1 cup nonfat cottage cheese
2 tablespoons butter
1 egg
1 tablespoon Splenda granular
¼ teaspoon baking soda
1 teaspoon salt
3 cups unbleached all-
    purpose or bread flour
1 package (2½ teaspoons)
    active dry yeast

**NUTRITIONAL ANALYSIS**
(per serving):

Calories: 81
Protein: 4 g
Carbohydrate: 13 g
Fat: 1 g
Sat. Fat: 1 g
Cholesterol: 12 mg
Sodium: 140 mg
Fiber: trace
Exchange Approx.:
1 Bread/Starch

# Hawaiian-Style Bread

**Yields 1 large loaf
(24 slices)
Serving size: 1 slice**

1 egg
½ cup pineapple juice (or ⅛
    cup frozen pineapple juice
    concentrate and ⅜ cup
    water)
¾ cup water
2 tablespoons butter
1 teaspoon vanilla*
½ teaspoon dried ginger
1 teaspoon salt
1½ cups unbleached bread
    flour
2⅛ cups unbleached all-
    purpose flour
¼ cup Splenda granular
2 tablespoons nonfat milk
    powder
1 package (2½ teaspoons)
    active dry yeast

**NUTRITIONAL ANALYSIS**
(per serving):

Calories: 90
Protein: 3 g
Carbohydrate: 16 g
Fat: 1 g
Sat. Fat: 1 g
Cholesterol: 11 mg
Sodium: 104 mg
Fiber: trace
Exchange Approx.:
1 Bread/Starch

*Vanilla extract contains a
trace amount of sugar. You
can substitute sugar-free
organic extract if you prefer.*

Unless the instructions for your bread machine
differ, add the ingredients in the order listed
here. Use the light-crust setting.

## Tools of the Trade

Nonstick pans with a dark surface absorb too
much heat, which causes breads to burn. Chi-
cago Metallic makes muffin, mini-muffin, and
other bread pans with a lighter-colored, Silver-
stone nonstick coating that are much better
suited for baking.

# Milk Biscuits

1. Preheat oven to 400°F. For quick mixing, use a food processor. Just add all of the ingredients at once and pulse until just blended. Be careful not to overprocess, as the rolls won't be as light.

2. To mix by hand, sift together the dry ingredients. Cut in the butter using a pastry blender or fork until the mixture resembles coarse crumbs. Add the milk and stir until the mixture pulls away from the sides of the bowl.

3. Use 1 heaping tablespoon for each biscuit, dropping the dough onto greased baking sheets. (You can also try pan liners, such as parchment.) Bake until golden brown, about 20 to 30 minutes. Despite the downside of all the butter, the upside to all the butter is that these biscuits are so rich you won't even notice that they don't contain any sugar. Consult your dietitian, however, if you are on a diet to control your cholesterol.

## Healthy Substitutions

You can substitute ¼ cup nonfat yogurt for half of the butter in this recipe.

**Yields 24 biscuits**
**Serving size: 1 biscuit**

3 cups unbleached all-
    purpose flour
1 teaspoon salt
1½ teaspoons baking soda
1 tablespoon cream of tartar
1 teaspoon baking powder
½ cup butter
1⅓ cups milk

**NUTRITIONAL ANALYSIS**
(per serving):

Calories: 98
Protein: 2 g
Carbohydrate: 13 g
Fat: 4 g
Sat. Fat: 3 g
Cholesterol: 11 mg
Sodium: 205 mg
Fiber: trace
Exchange Approx.:
1 Bread/Starch; ½ Fat

# Angelic Buttermilk Batter Biscuits

**Yields 24 biscuits**
**Serving size: 1 biscuit**

3 tablespoons nonfat
  buttermilk powder
2 tablespoons Splenda
  granular
¾ cup warm water
2½ cups unbleached all-
  purpose flour
1 tablespoon active dry yeast
½ teaspoon sea salt
½ teaspoon baking powder
¼ cup unsalted butter
¼ cup nonfat plain yogurt

**NUTRITIONAL ANALYSIS**
(per serving):

Calories: 71
Protein: 2 g
Carbohydrate: 11 g
Fat: 2 g
Sat. Fat: 1 g
Cholesterol: 6 mg
Sodium: 57 mg
Fiber: 1 g
Exchange Approx.:
1 Bread/Starch

1. Put the buttermilk powder, Splenda granular, and warm water in food processor and process until mixed. Sprinkle the yeast over the buttermilk-Splenda granular mixture and pulse once or twice to mix. Allow the mixture to sit at room temperature for about 5 minutes, or until the yeast begins to bubble. Add all the remaining ingredients to the food processor and pulse until mixed, being careful not to overprocess the dough.

2. Preheat oven to 400°F and drop 1 heaping teaspoon per biscuit onto a baking sheet treated with nonstick spray. Set the tray in a warm place and allow the biscuits to rise for about 15 minutes. Bake the biscuits for 12 to 15 minutes.

# Zucchini Bread

1. Preheat oven to 350°F. Treat two 9-inch loaf pans with nonstick spray. In a large bowl, beat the eggs until frothy. Beat in the Splenda granular, yogurt, and vanilla until thick and lemon-colored. Stir in the zucchini.

2. Sift together the flour, baking soda, baking powder, salt, and cinnamon. Stir dry ingredients into the zucchini batter. Fold in the nuts.

3. Pour the mixture into the prepared pans. Bake for 40 minutes, or until the center springs back when lightly touched. Allow to cool for 10 minutes before turning out onto a wire rack.

## Are Your Eyes Bigger Than Your Stomach?

Use miniloaf pans. It's much easier to arrive at the number of servings in the form of a full slice when you use smaller loaf pans. There's a psychological advantage to getting a full, rather than a half slice.

**Yields 2 large loaves**
**(20 slices)**
**Serving size: 1 slice**

3 eggs
1½ cups Splenda granular
1 cup nonfat plain yogurt
1 tablespoon vanilla*
2 cups, loosely packed, grated, unpeeled zucchini
2 cups unbleached all-purpose flour
2 teaspoons baking soda
½ teaspoon baking powder
1 teaspoon sea salt
1½ teaspoons cinnamon
1 cup chopped walnuts

**NUTRITIONAL ANALYSIS**
(per serving):

Calories: 110
Protein: 5 g
Carbohydrate: 214 g
Fat: 4 g
Sat. Fat: trace
Cholesterol: 32 mg
Sodium: 252 mg
Fiber: 1 g
Exchange Approx.:
1 Bread/Starch; 1
Carb./Sugar

*Vanilla extract contains a trace amount of sugar. You can substitute sugar-free organic extract if you prefer.

# Orange Date Bread

**Yields 4 mini loaves**
**Serving size: 1 slice**

2 tablespoons frozen orange
  juice concentrate
2 tablespoons orange zest
¾ cup pitted, chopped dates
½ cup honey
¼ cup Splenda granular
1 cup plain nonfat yogurt
1 egg
1¼ cups all-purpose flour
¾ cup whole-wheat flour
1 teaspoon baking soda
1 teaspoon baking powder
½ teaspoon salt
1 tablespoon vegetable oil
1 teaspoon vanilla extract *

1. Preheat oven to 350°F. Spray 4 mini-loaf pans with nonfat cooking spray. In a food processor, process the orange juice concentrate, orange zest, dates, honey, Splenda granular, yogurt, and egg until mixed. (This will cut the dates into smaller pieces, too.) Add the remaining ingredients and pulse until mixed, scraping down the side of the bowl if necessary.

2. Divide the mixture among the 4 pans. Spread the mixture so each pan has an even layer. Bake until a toothpick inserted into the center of a loaf comes out clean, about 15 to 20 minutes. Cool the bread in the pans on a wire rack for 10 minutes. Remove the bread to the rack and cool to room temperature.

**NUTRITIONAL ANALYSIS**
(per serving):

Calories: 55
Protein: 1 g
Carbohydrate: 12 g
Fat: 1 g
Sat. Fat: trace
Cholesterol: 5 mg
Sodium: 77 mg
Fiber: 1 g
Exchange Approx.:
1 Bread/Starch

*Vanilla extract contains a trace amount of sugar. You can substitute sugar-free organic extract if you prefer.

# Side Salads

## chapter eleven

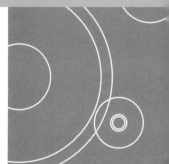

# Buttermilk Dressing

**Yields about ⅔ cup**
**Serving size: 1 tbs.**

½ cup plain nonfat yogurt
1 tablespoon buttermilk
 powder
1 teaspoon prepared mustard
¼ teaspoon cider vinegar
1 tablespoon honey
¼ teaspoon paprika
⅛ teaspoon hot red pepper
 (optional)
¼ teaspoon salt (optional)

The easiest way to make this fat-free dressing is to measure all the ingredients into a jar, then put the lid on the jar and shake it vigorously until it's mixed. Refrigerate any unused portions. May be kept in the refrigerator up to 3 days.

**NUTRITIONAL ANALYSIS**
(per serving, without salt):

Calories: 16
Protein: 1 g
Carbohydrate: 3 g
Fat: trace
Sat. Fat: trace
Cholesterol: 1 mg
Sodium: 72 mg
Fiber: trace
Exchange Approx.:
1 Free

# Bleu Cheese Dressing

Put the first 5 ingredients in a blender and process until smooth. Fold in the bleu cheese.

**Yields 6 tbs.**
**Serving size: 1 tbs.**

2 tablespoons Mock Sour
    Cream (see page 21)
1 tablespoons cottage cheese
1 tablespoon Hellmann's
    or Best Foods Real
    Mayonnaise
½ teaspoon lemon juice
½ teaspoon honey
1 tablespoon, plus 2
    teaspoons crumbled bleu
    cheese

**NUTRITIONAL ANALYSIS**
(per serving):

Calories: 24
Protein: 1 g
Carbohydrate: 1 g
Fat: 2 g
Sat. Fat: 1 g
Cholesterol: 3 mg
Sodium: 52 mg
Fiber: 0 g
Exchange Approx.:
½ Fat

# Dijon Vinaigrette

**Yields about 5 tbs.**
**Serving size: 1 tbs.**

1 tablespoon Dijon mustard
½ teaspoon sea salt
½ teaspoon freshly ground
   black pepper
1 tablespoon red wine vinegar
3 tablespoons virgin olive oil

**NUTRITIONAL ANALYSIS**
(per serving):

Calories: 74
Protein: trace
Carbohydrate: trace
Fat: 8 g
Sat. Fat: 1 g
Cholesterol: 0 mg
Sodium: 266 mg
Fiber: trace
Exchange Approx.:
2 Fats

Put all the ingredients in a small bowl and use a wire whisk or fork to mix.

# Honey-Mustard Dressing

Put all ingredients into a blender container or food processor and blend until smooth.

**Yields about ¾ cup**
**Serving size: 1 tbs.**

⅛ cup honey
1 clove garlic
2 tablespoons stone-ground mustard
1 tablespoon ground flaxseeds
1 teaspoon poppy seeds
1 tablespoon lemon juice
¼ cup flaxseed oil
1 tablespoon chopped fresh chives (or 1 teaspoon dried chives)
1 tablespoon toasted sesame seeds

## NUTRITIONAL ANALYSIS
(per serving):

Calories: 54
Protein: 1 g
Carbohydrate: 3 g
Fat: 4 g
Sat. Fat: trace
Cholesterol: 0 mg
Sodium: 25 mg
Fiber: 1 g
Exchange Approx.:
1 Fat

# Tangy Lemon-Garlic Tomato Dressing

**Yields about ¾ cup**
**Serving size: 1 tbs.**

1 tablespoon ground flaxseeds
2 cloves garlic
⅛ cup cider vinegar
⅛ teaspoon freshly ground
   pepper
1 small tomato, chopped
¼ teaspoon celery seed
1 tablespoon lemon juice
¼ cup water

---

**NUTRITIONAL ANALYSIS**
(per serving):

Calories: 7
Protein: trace
Carbohydrate: 1 g
Fat: trace
Sat. Fat: trace
Cholesterol: 0 mg
Sodium: 1 mg
Fiber: trace
Exchange Approx.:
½ Free

Place all ingredients in blender and blend until smooth.

## Friendly Fat and Fiber

In addition to providing fiber, ground flaxseeds are rich sources of omega-3 and -6 essential fatty acids. The oil is low in saturated fat, and therefore a heart-healthy choice. Just remember that flaxseed oil must be refrigerated; otherwise it goes rancid.

# Cashew-Garlic Ranch Dressing

Process the cashews and water together in a blender or food processor until creamy. Add the remaining ingredients and mix well. Refrigerate for 30 minutes.

## Keeping Cashews

Store raw cashews in the refrigerator; this preserves the healthy, but delicate, essential oils.

**Yields about ¾ cup**
**Serving size: 1 tbs.**

¼ cup raw cashews (or ⅛ cup cashew butter without salt)
½ cup water
½ teaspoon stone-ground mustard
1½ tablespoons chili sauce
½ teaspoon horseradish
1 teaspoon Bragg's Liquid Aminos (or tamari sauce)
1 clove garlic
1½ teaspoon honey
⅛ teaspoon pepper

**NUTRITIONAL ANALYSIS**
(per serving):

Calories: 21
Protein: 1 g
Carbohydrate: 2 g
Fat: 1 g
Sat. Fat: trace
Cholesterol: trace
Sodium: 14 mg
Fiber: trace
Exchange Approx.:
½ Fat

# Lemon-Almond Dressing

**Yields about ⅔ cup**
**Serving size: 1 tbs.**

¼ cup raw almonds
1 tablespoon lemon juice
¼ cup water
1½ teaspoons honey
¼ teaspoon lemon pepper
½ of a slice (1 inch in diameter) peeled ginger
¼ clove garlic
1½ teaspoons chopped, fresh chives (or ½ teaspoon dried chives)
1½ teaspoons chopped fresh sweet basil (or ½ teaspoon dried basil)

---

**NUTRITIONAL ANALYSIS**
(per serving):

Calories: 24
Protein: 1 g
Carbohydrate: 2 g
Fat: 2 g
Sat. Fat: trace
Cholesterol: 0 mg
Sodium: trace
Fiber: trace
Exchange Approx.:
½ Fat

Put all the ingredients in a food processor or blender and process until smooth.

## Salad: Undressed

Make a quick salad without dressing by mixing chopped celery, onion, and other vegetable choices such as cucumbers or zucchini. Add some of your favorite low-salt seasoning or toss the vegetables with some Bragg's Liquid Aminos or low-sodium soy sauce and serve over salad greens.

# Wilted Lettuce with a Healthier Difference

1. In a heated nonstick skillet treated with nonstick spray, add ½ teaspoon of the olive oil and all the red onion. Sauté until the onion is almost transparent, then add the greens. Sauté the greens until they're warmed and wilted.

2. In a salad bowl, whisk the lemon juice (or vinegar) with the ½ teaspoon of oil. Add the pinch of herbs and Splenda granular, if using, and whisk into the oil mixture. Add the wilted greens to the bowl and toss with the dressing. Top the salad with a pinch of toasted sesame seeds or Parmesan cheese, if desired. Serve immediately.

## Adventuresome Additions

Dried cranberries or other dried fruit, such as cherries or currants, are delicious in wilted lettuce dishes. The addition of diced apples or pineapple makes a perfect wilted greens accompaniment for pork. Have fun! Making necessary dietary changes isn't about learning a whole new way to cook. Adapting to a healthier new lifestyle is a chance to experiment.

**Serves 1**

½ teaspoon olive oil
¼ cup chopped red onion
1½ cups, tightly packed, loose-leaf lettuce
¼ teaspoon lemon juice or your choice of vinegar
½ teaspoon extra-virgin olive oil, walnut oil, or almond oil
Dried herbs of your choice, such as thyme or parsley
Pinch of Splenda granular
Pinch of toasted sesame seeds or grated Parmesan cheese

**NUTRITIONAL ANALYSIS**
(per serving):

Calories: 66
Protein: 1 g
Carbohydrate: 5 g
Fat: 5 g
Sat. Fat: 1 g
Cholesterol: 0 mg
Sodium: 8 mg
Fiber: 2 g
Exchange Approx.:
2 Free Vegetables,
1 Fat

# Greens in Garlic with Pasta

**Serves 4**

2 teaspoons olive oil
4 cloves garlic, crushed
6 cups, tightly packed, loose-leaf greens (baby mustard, turnip, chard)
2 cups cooked pasta
2 teaspoons extra-virgin olive oil
¼ cup freshly grated Parmesan cheese
Salt and freshly ground black pepper to taste (optional)

---

**NUTRITIONAL ANALYSIS**
(per serving, without salt):

Calories: 175
Protein: 8 g
Carbohydrate: 26 g
Fat: 5 g
Sat. Fat: 1 g
Cholesterol: trace
Sodium: 17 mg
Fiber: 3 g
Exchange Approx.: 1 Free Vegetable, 1 Fat, 1 Starch, ½ Lean Meat

1. Place a sauté pan over medium heat. When the pan is hot, add the 2 teaspoons of olive oil and the crushed garlic. Cook, stirring frequently until golden brown (3–5 minutes), being careful not to burn the garlic, as that makes it bitter. Add the greens and sauté until they are coated in the garlic oil. Remove from heat.

2. In a large serving bowl, add the pasta, cooked greens, 2 teaspoons of extra-virgin olive oil, and Parmesan cheese; toss to mix. Serve immediately, and season as desired.

## Sweet or Salty?

In most cases, when you add a pinch (less than ⅛ teaspoon) of Splenda granular to a recipe, you can reduce the amount of salt without noticing a difference. Splenda granular acts as a flavor enhancer and magnifies the effect of the salt.

# Green Bean and Mushroom Salad

1. Cook the green beans in a large pot of unsalted boiling water for 5 minutes. Drain the beans in a colander that you then immediately plunge into a bowl of ice water; this stops the cooking process and retains the bright green color of the beans.

2. Once the beans are cooled, drain and place in a large bowl. If you'll be serving the salad immediately, add the mushrooms and onions to the bowl and toss to mix. (Otherwise, as recommended earlier, chill the beans separately and add them to the salad immediately before serving.)

3. To make the dressing, combine the oil and vinegar in a small bowl. Whisk them together with the garlic and pour over the salad. Toss lightly and season with salt and pepper, if desired. Serve immediately.

**Serves 4**

2 cups fresh, small green beans, ends trimmed
1½ cups sliced, fresh mushrooms
½ cup chopped red onion
3 tablespoons extra-virgin olive, canola, or corn oil
1 tablespoon balsamic or red wine vinegar
1 clove garlic, minced
½ teaspoon sea salt (optional)
¼ teaspoon freshly ground pepper (optional)

---

## NUTRITIONAL ANALYSIS
(per serving):

Calories: 131
Protein: 2 g
Carbohydrate: 9 g
Fat: 10 g
Sat. Fat: 1 g
Cholesterol: 0 mg
Sodium: 4 mg
Fiber: 3 g
Exchange Approx.:
2 Fats, 2 Vegetables

# White and Black Bean Salad

**Serves 8**

1 cup finely chopped red
    onions
2 cloves garlic, minced
2 tablespoons olive oil or
    vegetable oil
⅓ cup red wine vinegar
¼ cup seeded and chopped
    red pepper
¼ cup seeded and chopped
    green pepper
2 tablespoons minced parsley
2 tablespoons Splenda
    granular
¼ teaspoon sea salt (optional)
¼ teaspoon pepper (optional)
1 (15-ounce) can Great
    Northern beans, rinsed and
    drained
1 (15-ounce) can black beans,
    rinsed and drained
Red and green pepper rings,
    for garnish

In a nonstick skillet over medium heat, sauté the onions and garlic in the oil until the onions are just beginning to soften. Remove from the heat and allow to cool until warm. Stir the vinegar, peppers, parsley, and Splenda granular into the onions and garlic. Pour the onion mixture over combined beans in a bowl and mix well. Season with salt and pepper, if desired, and garnish with pepper rings.

---

**NUTRITIONAL ANALYSIS**
(per serving):

Calories: 149
Protein: 7 g
Carbohydrate: 22 g
Fat: 4 g
Sat. Fat: 1 g
Cholesterol: 0 mg
Sodium: 226 mg
Fiber: 6 g
Exchange Approx.:
1 Misc. Carb., 1 Fat,
1 Starch

186

# Broccoli-Cauliflower Slaw

Put the broccoli and cauliflower in a food processor and pulse-process to the consistency of shredded cabbage; pour into a bowl. Place the remaining ingredients in the food processor and process until smooth. Pour the resulting dressing over the broccoli-cauliflower mixture and stir. Chill until ready to serve.

## Fresh Herb Conversions

If you substitute dried herbs for the fresh ones called for in a recipe, only use ⅓ the amount.

**Serves 8**

4 cups raw broccoli flowerets
4 cups raw cauliflower
½ cup Hellmann's or Best Foods Real Mayonnaise
1 cup cottage cheese, 1% fat
3 tablespoons tarragon vinegar
1 tablespoon balsamic vinegar
⅛ cup honey
3 tablespoons red onion

**NUTRITIONAL ANALYSIS**
(per serving):

Calories: 160
Protein: 6 g
Carbohydrate: 10 g
Fat: 12 g
Sat. Fat: 2 g
Cholesterol: 6 mg
Sodium: 218 mg
Fiber: 2 g
Exchange Approx.:
1 Misc. Carb., 1 Fat

# Zesty Feta and Olive Salad

**Serves 4**

2 ounces crumbled feta
1 small red onion, diced
½ cup chopped celery
½ cup diced cucumber
1 clove garlic, minced
1 teaspoon lemon zest
1 teaspoon orange zest
1 cup halved, very small
    cherry tomatoes
½ cup mix of green and
    kalamata olives, pitted and
    sliced
1 tablespoon extra-virgin
    olive oil
2 tablespoons minced fresh
    Italian parsley
2 teaspoons minced fresh
    oregano
1 teaspoon minced fresh mint
1 tablespoon minced fresh
    cilantro (optional)
Large romaine or butter
    lettuce leaves
Freshly ground black pepper

Place the feta in a large bowl and add the onion, celery, cucumber, garlic, lemon zest, orange zest, cherry tomatoes, and olives; mix. Add the olive oil and fresh herbs and toss again. Arrange the lettuce leaves on 4 salad plates and spoon the feta salad on top. Top with freshly ground pepper, and serve.

**NUTRITIONAL ANALYSIS**
(per serving):

Calories: 109
Protein: 3 g
Carbohydrate: 6 g
Fat: 8 g
Sat. Fat: 3 g
Cholesterol: 13 mg
Sodium: 327 mg
Fiber: 2 g
Exchange Approx.: 1
Vegetable, 2 Fats

# Avocado and Peach Salad

In a measuring cup, whisk the water, orange juice concentrate, garlic, vinegar, oil, and vanilla together until well mixed. Prepare the salad by arranging layers of the arugula and tarragon, then the avocado, peach, and onions, and then drizzle the salad with the orange juice vinaigrette. Season with salt and pepper, if desired, and serve.

## Experiment Sensibly

When it comes to new herbs and spices, err on the side of caution. If you're not sure whether or not you like a seasoning, mix all of the other ingredients together and "test" a bite of the salad with a pinch of the herb or spice before you add it to the entire recipe.

**Serves 4**

⅛ cup water
⅛ cup frozen unsweetened orange juice concentrate
1 clove garlic, crushed
1 teaspoon rice wine vinegar
1 tablespoon extra-virgin olive oil
½ teaspoon vanilla*
1½ cups, tightly packed, baby arugula
2 tablespoons tarragon leaves
1 avocado, peeled and diced
1 peach, peeled and diced
½ cup thinly sliced Vidalia onion
Kosher or sea salt and freshly ground black pepper to taste (optional)

**NUTRITIONAL ANALYSIS**
(per serving, without salt):

Calories: 160
Protein: 2 g
Carbohydrate: 15 g
Fat: 11 g
Sat. Fat: 2 g
Cholesterol: 0 mg
Sodium: 11 mg
Fiber: 4 g
Exchange Approx.: 3 Fats, 1 Free Vegetable, ½ Fruit

*Vanilla extract contains a trace amount of sugar. You can substitute sugar-free organic extract if you prefer.

# Orange-Avocado Slaw

**Serves 10**

¼ cup unsweetened orange
    juice
½ teaspoon curry powder
⅛ teaspoon ground cumin
¼ teaspoon Splenda granular
1 teaspoon white wine vinegar
1 tablespoon olive oil
5 cups broccoli slaw mix
1 avocado, peeled and
    chopped
Sea salt and freshly ground
    black pepper to taste
    (optional)

In a bowl, whisk together the orange juice,
curry powder, cumin, Splenda granular, and
vinegar. Add the oil in a stream, whisking until
emulsified. In a large bowl, toss the avocado
with the slaw mix. Drizzle with the vinaigrette.
Chill until ready to serve, and season with salt
and pepper, if desired.

**NUTRITIONAL ANALYSIS**
(per serving, without salt):

Calories: 59.87
Protein: 1.78 g
Carbohydrate: 4.55 g
Fat: 4.60 g
Sat. Fat: 0.70 g
Cholesterol: 0 mg
Sodium: 14.01 mg
Fiber: 2.34 g
Exchange Approx.: 1
Fat, ½ Free Vegetable

# Honey Dijon Tuna Salad

1. Use a fork to flake the tuna into a bowl. Add all the other ingredients except the lettuce and mix well. Serve on lettuce or greens.

2. Alternate serving suggestion: Mix with ½ cup of chilled, cooked pasta before dressing the salad greens; adds 1 Starch Exchange choice.

**Serves 1**

¼ cup tuna, canned in water, drained
½ cup diced celery
¼ cup diced onion
¼ cup seeded and diced red or green pepper
4 ounces (half of a small container) nonfat plain yogurt
1 teaspoon Dijon mustard
1 teaspoon lemon juice
¼ teaspoon honey
1 tablespoon raisins
1 cup, tightly packed, iceberg lettuce (or other salad greens)

**NUTRITIONAL ANALYSIS**
(per serving):

Calories: 194
Protein: 22 g
Carbohydrate: 24 g
Fat: 1 g
Sat. Fat: trace
Cholesterol: 0 mg
Sodium: 575 mg
Fiber: 4 g
Exchange Approx.:
1 Lean Meat, 2 Vegetables, ½ Fruit, ½ Skim Milk

# Spinach Salad with Apple-Avocado Dressing

**Serves 4**

¼ cup unsweetened apple juice

1 teaspoon (or up to 1 tablespoon) cider vinegar

1 clove garlic, minced

1 teaspoon Bragg's Liquid Aminos or soy sauce

½ teaspoon Worcestershire sauce (see recipe for Homemade on page 17)

2 teaspoons olive oil

1 avocado, peeled and chopped

2½ cups, tightly packed, spinach and other salad greens

½ cup thinly sliced red onion

½ cup sliced radishes

½ cup bean sprouts

---

**NUTRITIONAL ANALYSIS**

(per serving):

Calories: 128

Protein: 2 g

Carbohydrate: 10 g

Fat: 10 g

Sat. Fat: 2 g

Cholesterol: 0 mg

Sodium: 102 mg

Fiber: 3 g

Exchange Approx.: 2½ Fats, 1 Free Vegetable

In a blender or food processor, combine the juice, vinegar (the amount of which will depend on how you like your dressing), garlic, Liquid Aminos (or soy sauce), Worcestershire, oil, and avocado; process until smooth. In a large bowl, toss the salad ingredients. Pour the dressing over the salad and toss again.

## Salads Don't Have to Be Fat Free

Unless you're on a calorie-restricted diet, "fat-free" may not be your best choice—consult your dietitian. Studies show that women who consume up to 41.7 grams of vegetable fat a day have up to a 22 percent less change of developing type 2 diabetes. Vegetable oils—combined with a diet rich in fish, fruits, vegetables, whole grains, and nuts—are much healthier than using those chemically created fat-free foods! This type of diet is not only heart-healthy, it's believed to prevent certain cancers, too. (Source: WebMD, *http://my.webmd.com*)

# Greek Pasta Salad

In a large salad bowl, whisk the lemon juice together with the olive oil, oregano, mustard, and garlic. Cover and refrigerate for 1 hour, or up to 12 hours. Immediately before serving, toss the pasta with the almonds, cucumbers, tomatoes, red onions, olives, and feta cheese. Serve over the lettuce.

## Sweet and Savory Side Salad

For 1 serving of an easy, versatile salad or a simple dressing over salad greens, mix ¾ cup shredded carrots, ¼ cup diced celery, 1 table-spoon raisins, and 1 teaspoon frozen pineapple juice concentrate. The Nutritional Analysis is: Calories: 31; Protein: trace g; Carbohydrate: 8 g; Fat: 1 g; Sat. Fat: trace g; Cholesterol: 0 mg; Sodium: 15 mg; Fiber: 1 g; PCF Ratio: 6-92-2. Exchange Approximations: ½ Fruit, 1 Free Vegetable, 1 Vegetable.

**Serves 4**

1 tablespoon lemon juice
3 tablespoons olive oil
1 teaspoon dried oregano
1 teaspoon Dijon mustard
1 clove garlic, minced
2 cups cooked pasta
1 cup slivered, blanched almonds
1 cup sliced cucumber
1 cup diced fresh tomato
½ cup chopped red onion
½ cup Greek olives
2 ounces crumbled feta cheese
1½ cups romaine lettuce leaves

**NUTRITIONAL ANALYSIS**
(per serving):

Calories: 420
Protein: 12 g
Carbohydrate: 31 g
Fat: 29 g
Sat. Fat: 5 g
Cholesterol: 13 mg
Sodium: 312 mg
Fiber: 6 g
Exchange Approx.:
1 Medium-Fat Meat,
1 Meat Substitute,
1 Free Vegetable,
1½ Starches, 4 Fats

# Bleu Cheese Pasta Salad

**Serves 4**

1 recipe Bleu Cheese Pasta
  (see page 132)
4 cups, tightly packed, salad
  greens
4 slices red onion
4 ounces thinly sliced or
  chopped chicken breast,
  broiled, grilled, or steamed
18 large black olives, sliced
Nonstarchy vegetables of
  your choice, such as sliced
  cucumbers, tomato, or
  zucchini to taste (optional)

---

**NUTRITIONAL ANALYSIS**
(per serving):

Calories: 281
Protein: 21 g
Carbohydrate: 24 g
Fat: 11 g
Sat. Fat: 5 g
Cholesterol: 38 mg
Sodium: 402 mg
Fiber: 2 g
Exchange Approx.:
½ High Fat Meat,
1½ Very Lean Meats,
½ Lean Meat, 1 Carb./
Starch, 1 Fat

Prepare the Bleu Cheese Pasta (warm or chilled). Divide the salad greens between 4 plates. Top each salad with a slice of red onion, the olives, 1 ounce of the chicken breast, and the free exchange vegetables of your choice, if desired. Top with the pasta.

# Taco Salad

Prepare the Vegetable and Bean Chili. Divide the salad greens between 8 large bowls. Top with the chili, Cheddar cheese, corn chips, and vegetables or peppers, if using.

**Serves 8**

1 recipe Vegetable and Bean
  Chili (see page 141)
8 cups, tightly packed, salad
  greens
8 ounces Cheddar cheese,
  shredded (to yield 2 cups)
8 ounces nonfat corn chips
Nonstarchy free exchange
  vegetables of your choice,
  such as chopped celery,
  onion, or banana or
  jalapeno peppers (optional)

**NUTRITIONAL ANALYSIS**
(per serving):

Calories: 426
Protein: 23 g
Carbohydrate: 58 g
Fat: 13 g
Sat. Fat: 7 g
Cholesterol: 30 mg
Sodium: 380 mg
Fiber: 13 g
Exchange Approx.:
1 Lean Meat, 1 High
Fat Meat, 3 Starches,
2 Vegetables

# Layered Salad

**Serves 6**

¼ cup Hellmann's or Best Foods Real Mayonnaise
1¼ cups nonfat cottage cheese
½ cup nonfat plain yogurt
1 tablespoon apple cider vinegar or lemon juice
1 tablespoon Splenda granular
6 cups shredded mixed lettuce
1½ cups diced celery
1½ cups chopped onion, any variety
1½ cups sliced carrots
1½ cups frozen green peas, thawed
6 ounces (2 percent fat or less) smoked turkey breast
6 ounces Cheddar cheese, shredded (to yield 1½ cups)

---

**NUTRITIONAL ANALYSIS**
(per serving):

Calories: 318
Protein: 23 g
Carbohydrate: 20 g
Fat: 18 g
Sat. Fat: 7 g
Cholesterol: 48 mg
Sodium: 697 mg
Fiber: 5 g
Exchange Approx.:
1 High-Fat Meat, 1 Lean Meat, 1 Vegetable, 2 Fats

1. Combine the mayonnaise, cottage cheese, yogurt, vinegar (or lemon juice), and Splenda granular in a food processor or blender; process until smooth. Set aside.

2. In a large salad bowl, layer the lettuce, celery, onion, carrots, peas, and turkey breast. Spread the mayonnaise mixture "dressing" over the top of the salad. Top with the shredded cheese.

## Yogurt-Mayo Sandwich Spread

Spread a little flavor! Measure ½ teaspoon drained nonfat yogurt into a paper coffee filter. Twist to secure; drain over a cup or bowl in the refrigerator for at least 1 hour. In a small bowl, combine the drained yogurt with ½ teaspoon Hellmann's or Best Foods Real Mayonnaise. Use as you would mayonnaise. A 1-teaspoon serving has: Calories: 12; Protein: trace g; Carbohydrate: 1 g; Fat: 1 g; Sat. Fat: trace g; Cholesterol: 1 mg; Sodium: 20 mg; Fiber: 0 g; PCF Ratio: 8-29-63. Exchange Approximations: 1 Free Condiment.

# Golden Raisin Smoked Turkey Salad

Combine the broccoli, cauliflower, and shallots in a large bowl and stir in the raisins. In a blender or food processor, mix together the cottage cheese, mayonnaise, tofu, vinegars, honey, and pepper until smooth. Toss the dressing over the broccoli, cauliflower, raisins, shallots, and turkey. Season with freshly ground pepper to taste. Chill until ready to serve, over salad greens.

## Just How Bad Is Bacon?

According to a Nutritional Analysis done by Cybersoft, Inc. (makers of the NutriBase 2001 software), when bacon is cooked until it's crisp—and drained to remove as much fat as possible, it still adds a whopping 732 calories! That comes out to about 39 grams of protein and 63 grams of fat, a third of which are from saturated fats (the bad guys).

**Yields 4 generous-sized salads**

4 cups chopped broccoli
2 cups chopped cauliflower
3 shallots, chopped
1⅓ cups golden raisins
1 cup 1% cottage cheese
¼ cup Hellmann's or Best Foods Real Mayonnaise
¼ cup firm silken tofu
3 tablespoons tarragon vinegar
1 tablespoon balsamic vinegar
¼ cup honey
¼ pound (4 ounces) smoked turkey breast, chopped
Freshly ground pepper (optional)
4 cups salad greens

**NUTRITIONAL ANALYSIS**
(per serving):

Calories: 455
Protein: 19 g
Carbohydrate: 74 g
Fat: 14 g
Sat. Fat: 2 g
Cholesterol: 20 mg
Sodium: 603 mg
Fiber: 6 g
Exchange Approx.:
1 Very Lean Meat, 1 Lean Meat, 1½ Vegetables, 3 Fats, 1 Fruit, 1 Misc. Carb.

# Desserts and Goodies

## chapter twelve

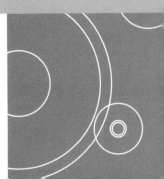

# Individual Sponge Cakes

**Yields 12 cupcakes**
**Serving size: 1 cupcake**

1 cup flour
½ teaspoon salt
1 teaspoon baking powder
3 eggs
¾ cup Splenda granular
1 tablespoon lemon juice
6 tablespoons hot milk
½ teaspoon lemon zest
(optional)

**NUTRITIONAL ANALYSIS**
(per serving):

Calories: 68
Protein: 3 g
Carbohydrate: 10 g
Fat: 2 g
Sat. Fat: 1 g
Cholesterol: 54 mg
Sodium: 151 mg
Fiber: trace
Exchange Approx.:
1½ Breads/Starches

1. Preheat oven to 350°F. Mix together the flour, salt, and baking powder. In a food processor or mixing bowl, beat the eggs until fluffy and lemon colored. Add the Splenda granular, lemon juice, and, if using, the lemon zest. Add the flour mixture; process only enough to blend. Add the hot milk and process until blended.

2. Pour into a 12-section muffin pan treated with nonstick spray. (Also works well as 24 mini-muffins.) If lining the muffin pan, use foil liners. Bake for 15 minutes, or until a toothpick inserted in the center of a cupcake comes out clean. The cakes will be golden brown and firm to the touch. Move the cupcakes to a rack to cool.

## Snack Cakes

Use a pastry bag to "pump" some nonfat whipped topping or sugar-free jelly (or a mixture of the 2) into the center of the Individual Sponge Cakes, and you have a healthier, homemade snack cake alternative.

# Glazed Carrot Cake

1. Preheat oven to 350°F. Sift together the dry ingredients and spices. Using a food processor or mixer, blend together the Splenda granular, apple juice concentrate, and eggs until well mixed. Stir the water and ground flaxseed together in a small microwave-safe bowl and microwave on high for 30 seconds; stir. (Mixture should be the consistency of egg whites; if it hasn't thickened to that appearance, microwave at 15-second increments until it does.) Gradually beat into the egg mixture, along with the vanilla, yogurt, and the ¼ cup pineapple liquid. Stir in the dry ingredients. Fold the crushed pineapple (drained of any remaining juice), shredded carrots, and raisins.

2. Treat an 8-inch baking pan with nonstick spray. Spoon the mixture into the pan, then bake for 20 to 25 minutes. Allow the cake to cool slightly while you prepare the glaze.

3. Mix the apple juice concentrate and water until the concentrate is melted. (You can microwave the mixture for 15 to 20 seconds, if necessary.) Spread evenly over the cake.

*Vanilla extract contains a trace amount of sugar. You can substitute sugar-free organic extract if you prefer.*

**Serves 9**

½ cups unbleached flour
1 teaspoon baking powder
1 teaspoon baking soda
1½ teaspoons cinnamon
¼ teaspoon ground cloves
¼ teaspoon ground allspice
⅛ teaspoon ground nutmeg
1 tablespoon Splenda granular
⅛ cup (2 tbsp) frozen, unsweetened apple juice concentrate
2 eggs
¼ cup water
2 tbsp ground flaxseed
1 teaspoon vanilla*
3 tbsp nonfat plain yogurt
1 cup canned, unsweetened crushed pineapple, ¼ cup of liquid retained
1 cup finely shredded carrots
¼ cup seedless raisins
Glaze
⅛ cup (2 tablespoons) frozen, unsweetened apple juice concentrate
1 tablespoon water

**NUTRITIONAL ANALYSIS**
(per serving):

Calories: 152
Protein: 5 g
Carbohydrate: 29 g
Fat: 2 g
Sat. Fat: trace
Cholesterol: 47 mg
Sodium: 222 mg
Fiber: 2 g
Exchange Approx.:
1 Bread/Starch, ½ Vegetable, 1 Fruit

# Mock Whipped Cream

**Yields 3½ cups**
**Serving size: 2 tbs.**

1 envelope KNOX Unflavored
  Gelatine
¼ cup cold water
½ cup hot water
2 tablespoons almond oil
3 tablespoons Splenda
  granular
1 teaspoon vanilla*
1 cup ice water
1¼ cups nonfat milk powder

---

**NUTRITIONAL ANALYSIS**
(per serving):

Calories: 21
Protein: 1 g
Carbohydrate: 2 g
Fat: 1 g
Sat. Fat: trace
Cholesterol: 1 mg
Sodium: 18 mg
Fiber: 0 g
Exchange Approx.:
½ Fat

*Vanilla extract contains a
trace amount of sugar.
You can substitute sugar-
free organic extract if you
prefer.

1. Allow the gelatin to soften in the cold water, then pour the mixture into a blender. Add the hot water and blend for 2 minutes until the gelatin is dissolved.

2. While continuing to blend the mixture, gradually add the almond oil and Splenda. Chill in the freezer for 15 minutes, or until the mixture is cool but hasn't yet begun to "set."

3. Using a hand mixer or whisk, add the ice water and nonfat milk powder to a chilled bowl and beat until peaks start to form. Gradually add vanilla. Add the gelatin mixture to the whipped milk and continue to whip until stiffer peaks begin to form. This whipped topping will keep several days in the refrigerator. Whip again to reintroduce more air into the topping before serving.

TIP: There is some fat in this recipe, but the use of vegetable (almond) oil reduces the Saturated Fat and Cholesterol Amounts considerably compared to making whipped cream using real cream.

# Date-Nut Roll

1. Place graham crackers in a plastic bag and use a rolling pin to crush them or process into crumbs in a food processor. Mix the resulting graham cracker crumbs with the chopped walnuts and dates.

2. Gently fold in the Mock Whipped Cream. Turn the mixture out onto a piece of aluminum foil (if you plan to freeze it) or onto plastic wrap (if you'll only be chilling it until you're ready to serve it).

3. Shape the mixture into a log shape and wrap securely in the foil or plastic wrap. Chill for at least 4 hours before serving. Cut into 12 slices.

**Serves 12**

12 graham crackers
¼ cup finely chopped walnuts
12 dates, chopped
¼ cup Mock Whipped Cream
(see page 202)

---

**NUTRIENT ANALYSIS**

(per serving):

Calories: 72
Protein: 2 g
Carbohydrate: 13 g
Fat: 2 g
Sat. Fat: trace
Cholesterol: trace
Sodium: 49 mg
Fiber: 1 g
Exchange Approx.:
1 Fat, ½ Bread/Starch,
½ Fruit

# Chocolate Cheesecake Mousse

**Serves 4**

¾ cup Mock Whipped Cream
 (see page 202)
1 tablespoon chopped sugar-
 free dark chocolate
1 ounce cream cheese
1½ teaspoons unsweetened
 cocoa
1 teaspoon vanilla*

*Vanilla extract contains a
trace amount of sugar.
You can substitute sugar-
free organic extract if you
prefer.*

1. Put the chocolate and 1 tablespoon of the Mock Whipped Cream in a microwave-safe bowl and microwave on high for 15 seconds. Add the cream cheese to the bowl and micro-wave on high for another 15 seconds.

2. Whip the mixture until it is well blended and the chocolate is melted. Stir in the cocoa and vanilla. Fold in the remaining Mock Whipped Cream. Chill until ready to serve.

# Chocolate Cheesecake Mousse II

1. Put the chocolate in a microwave-safe bowl along with about ¼ cup of the Whipped Milk Base. Microwave on high for 20 seconds. Beat vigorously with a fork or whisk until the chocolate is melted and blended in with the milk. If necessary, microwave on high for another 5 to 10 seconds.

2. The mixture will be very warm at this point. Cut the cream cheese into several pieces, each about 1 tablespoon in size, and add it to the chocolate mixture. Beat vigorously until the cream cheese is blended into the chocolate. Add the vanilla and stir to mix. Pour the mixture into the remaining Whipped Milk Base, using a spatula to scrape the sides of the bowl. Chill for at least 1 hour before serving.

*TIP: To compensate for the difference in whipped textures, this recipe uses more chocolate, so the calories per serving are higher than in the recipe on page 230.*

**Serves 12**

4 ounces chopped sugar-free dark chocolate
1 recipe Nonfat Whipped Milk Base (see page 206)
4 ounces cream cheese, at room temperature
1 teaspoon vanilla*

---

**NUTRITIONAL ANALYSIS**
(per serving):

Calories: 100
Protein: 4 g
Carbohydrate: 5 g
Fat: 9 g
Sat. Fat: 5 g
Cholesterol: 11 mg
Sodium: 29 mg
Fiber: 1 g
Exchange Approx.:
1 Skim Milk, ½ Fat

*Vanilla extract contains a trace amount of sugar. You can substitute sugar-free organic extract if you prefer.

# Nonfat Whipped Milk Base

**Yields about 3 cups**

¼ cup nonfat milk powder
⅛ cup Splenda granular
1 cup chilled skim milk, divided
1½ envelopes KNOX Unflavored Gelatine

---

**NUTRITIONAL ANALYSIS**
(per recipe):

Calories: 194
Protein: 23 g
Carbohydrate: 24 g
Fat: 1 g
Sat. Fat: trace
Cholesterol: 10.78 mg
Sodium: 310.68 mg
Fiber: 0 g
Exchange Approx.:
2 Skim Milks, 1 Carb.

1. In a chilled bowl, combine the milk powder and Splenda granular, and mix until well blended. Pour ¼ cup of the chilled skim milk and the gelatine into a blender; let sit for 1 or 2 minutes for the gelatine to soften.

2. In a microwave-safe container, heat the remaining skim milk until it almost reaches the boiling point, or about 30 to 45 seconds on high. Add the heated milk to the blender with the gelatine, and blend for 2 minutes, or until the gelatine is completely dissolved. Chill for 15 minutes or until the mixture is cool, but the gelatine hasn't yet begun to "set."

3. Using a hand mixer or a whisk, beat the mixture until it's doubled in size. (It won't form stiff peaks like whipped cream; however, you'll notice that it'll get a creamier white in color.) Chill until ready to use in one of the next desserts. If necessary, whip again immediately prior to folding in the other mousse ingredients.

*TIP: For best results, chill a glass bowl in the freezer for 1 hour for use in preparing this recipe.*

## Whipping Methods

Because you don't need to whip the Whipped Milk Base until it reaches stiff peaks, you can use a blender or food processor; however, you won't be whipping as much air into the mixture if you do, so the serving sizes will be a bit smaller.

# Orange Marmalade Cheesecake Mousse

In a microwave-safe bowl, heat the orange marmalade and cream cheese for 15 seconds. Whip until well blended. Gently fold in the Mock Whipped Cream and vanilla. Chill until ready to serve.

**Serves 4**

⅞ cup Mock Whipped Cream (see page 202)
⅛ cup, plus 2 teaspoons sugar-free orange marmalade
1 ounce cream cheese
1 teaspoon vanilla extract*

---

**NUTRITIONAL ANALYSIS**
(per serving):

Calories: 75
Protein: 4 g
Carbohydrate: 14 g
Fat: 4 g
Sat. Fat: 2 g
Cholesterol: 10 mg
Sodium: 86 mg
Fiber: 0 g
Exchange Approx.:
½ Skim Milk, ½ Fat

*Vanilla extract contains a trace amount of sugar. You can substitute sugar-free organic extract if you prefer.*

# Peanut Butter Pleaser

**Serves 4**

⅞ cups Mock Whipped Cream
(see page 202)
1 teaspoon vanilla extract*
1 tablespoon, plus 1 teaspoon
unsalted, smooth peanut
butter

**NUTRITIONAL ANALYSIS**
(per serving):

Calories: 77
Protein: 5 g
Carbohydrate: 12 g
Fat: 4 g
Sat. Fat: 1 g
Cholesterol: 2 mg
Sodium: 90 mg
Fiber: trace
Exchange Approx.:
½ Skim Milk, ½ Fat

*Vanilla extract contains a
trace amount of sugar.
You can substitute sugar-
free organic extract if you
prefer.

In a bowl, fold the peanut butter and vanilla
into the Mock Whipped Cream until well
blended. Chill until ready to serve.

# Whipped Lemon Cheesecake Mousse

In a small bowl, combine the cream cheese, lemon juice and zest, and Splenda granular; using a fork or whisk, beat until well blended. Fold the mixture into the Whipped Milk Base. Chill for at least 1 hour before serving.

**Serves 10**

4 ounces cream cheese, room temperature
1 tablespoon lemon juice
1 teaspoon lemon zest
¼ cup Splenda granular
1 recipe Whipped Milk Base (see page 206)

**NUTRITIONAL ANALYSIS**
(per serving):

Calories: 62
Protein: 3 g
Carbohydrate: 3 g
Fat: 4 g
Sat. Fat: 2 g
Cholesterol: 13 mg
Sodium: 34 mg
Fiber: trace
Exchange Approx.:
1 Skim Milk

# Whipped Mocha Mousse

**Serves 10**

¼ cup cold water
1 envelope KNOX Unflavored
   Gelatine
¾ cup hot water
2 teaspoons instant espresso
   powder
½ cup Splenda granular
¼ cup unsweetened cocoa
1½ teaspoons vanilla extract*
1 recipe Whipped Milk Base
   (see page 206)
Ground cinnamon (optional)

(see page 206)

1. Pour the cold water into a blender and sprinkle the unflavored gelatine over it; let stand for 1 minute.

2. Add the hot water and instant espresso powder, and blend at low speed until the gelatin is completely dissolved. Add the Splenda granular, cocoa, and vanilla; process at high speed until blended. Allow the mixture to cool to at least room temperature before folding it into the Whipped Milk Base. Chill until ready to serve.

**NUTRITIONAL ANALYSIS**
(per serving):

Calories: 47
Protein: 4 g
Carbohydrate: 7 g
Fat: trace
Sat. Fat: trace
Cholesterol: 1 mg
Sodium: 34 mg
Fiber: 1 g
Exchange Approx.:
1 Skim Milk

*Vanilla extract contains a trace amount of sugar. You can substitute sugar-free organic extract if you prefer.*

# Carrot-Fruit Cup

1. Soak the raisins overnight in a little more than enough water to cover them.

2. When you're ready to prepare the dessert, drain the water from the raisins and pour them into a bowl. Add the carrots and apple. Stir in the frozen apple juice concentrate and spices until blended. Add the banana slices and stir again. Chill until ready to serve.

**Serves 4**

1 tablespoon raisins
2 carrots, grated
1 apple, grated
1 tablespoon frozen apple
  juice concentrate
1 teaspoon cinnamon
Pinch of ginger
1 frozen banana, sliced

**NUTRITIONAL ANALYSIS**
(per serving):

Calories: 69
Protein: 1 g
Carbohydrate: 18 g
Fat: trace
Sat. Fat: trace
Cholesterol: 0 mg
Sodium: 13 mg
Fiber: 2 g
Exchange Approx.:
1 Fruit, ½ Vegetable

# Lucky Lemonade Gelatin

**Serves 4**

1 envelope KNOX Unflavored
Gelatine
¼ cup cold water
1½ cups hot water
¼ cup fresh lemon juice (or
lime juice)
3 tablespoons sugar-free
orange marmalade
1 tablespoon Splenda granular

1. In a blender container, soak the gelatine in the cold water for 2 minutes, then add the hot water and blend for about 2 minutes, or until the gelatine is dissolved.

2. Add the juice, marmalade, and Splenda granular, and blend until the Splenda granular is dissolved. Pour into a dish or mold and refrigerate until set, about 3 hours, or longer.

**NUTRITIONAL ANALYSIS**
(per serving):

Calories: 19
Protein: 2 g
Carbohydrate: 5 g
Fat: 0 g
Sat. Fat: 0 g
Cholesterol: 0 mg
Sodium: 7 mg
Fiber: trace
Exchange Approx.:
1 Fruit

# Faux Chocolate Bavarian Cream

1. While you soak the gelatine in the cold water (for at least 3 minutes), heat the 1½ cups of skim milk in a saucepan over medium heat just until bubbles begin to form around the edge. Turn the heat as low as it will go, and add the milk powder, cocoa, and Splenda granular; stir until they dissolve. Add the hot water to the gelatine, and stir until the gelatine dissolves. Add the gelatine to the milk mixture and stir well. Refrigerate until set, at least 3 hours.

2. Once the gelatine has set completely, put it in a blender with the remaining 2 table-spoons of skim milk. Blend until the mixture has a pudding-like consistency. If necessary, add more milk.

*TIP: This cream is best served right away, but if you have to wait, give it a quick blend just beforehand to mix in any ingredients that may have separated out.*

**Serves 4**

1 envelope KNOX Unflavored Gelatine
⅛ cup cold water
1½ cups skim milk, plus 2 tablespoons
¼ cup nonfat milk powder
2 tablespoons unsweetened cocoa
4 teaspoons Splenda granular
⅛ cup hot water

---

**NUTRITIONAL ANALYSIS**
(per serving):

Calories: 61
Protein: 7 g
Carbohydrate: 9 g
Fat: 1 g
Sat. Fat: trace
Cholesterol: 2 mg
Sodium: 75 mg
Fiber: 1 g
Exchange Approx.:
1 Skim Milk

# Bubbly Berry Blast

**Serves 6**

2 envelopes KNOX Unflavored
  Gelatine
½ cup frozen, unsweetened
  apple juice concentrate
3 cups (24 ounces)
  unsweetened sparkling
  water
1 cup sliced strawberries
1 cup blueberries

## NUTRITIONAL ANALYSIS
(per serving):

Calories: 61
Protein: 2 g
Carbohydrate: 13 g
Fat: trace
Sat. Fat: trace
Cholesterol: 0 mg
Sodium: 11 mg
Fiber: 1 g
Exchange Approx.:
1 Fruit

1. Mix the gelatine and apple juice in a small saucepan, stir, and let stand for 1 minute. Place the mixture over low heat and stir until completely dissolved, about 3 minutes. Cool slightly. (Alternatively, blend the gelatine and apple juice in a small, microwave-safe bowl, let stand 1 minute, and then microwave on high for 45 seconds; stir mixture until the gelatine is completely dissolved.) Stir in the sparkling water. Refrigerate until mixture begins to gel or is the consistency of unbeaten egg whites when stirred.

2. Fold the fruit into the partially thickened gelatine mixture. Pour into a 6-cup mold. Refrigerate for 4 hours, or until firm.

# Baked Pear Crisp

1. Preheat oven to 375°F. Treat a 9" × 13" baking dish or large, flat casserole dish with non-stick cooking spray. Core and cut up the pears into the baking dish. (Except for any bruised spots; it's okay to leave the skins on.)

2. In a glass measuring cup, microwave the frozen juice concentrate for 1 minute. Stir in the vanilla and rum, then pour over the pears. Using the same measuring cup, microwave the butter 30-40 seconds until melted. Toss the remaining ingredients together in a bowl, being careful not to crush the cereal. Spread uniformly over the pears and dribble the melted butter over the top of the cereal. Bake for 35 minutes, or until the mixture is bubbling and the top is just beginning to brown. Serve hot or cold.

**Serves 4**

2 pears
2 tablespoons frozen, unsweetened pineapple juice concentrate
1 teaspoon vanilla extract*
1 teaspoon rum
1 tablespoon butter
⅛ cup Ener-G Brown Rice Flour
⅓ cup, firmly packed Splenda granular
½ cup oat bran flakes

**NUTRITIONAL ANALYSIS**
(per serving):

Calories: 152
Protein: 3 g
Carbohydrate: 30 g
Fat: 4 g
Sat. Fat: 2 g
Cholesterol: 8 mg
Sodium: 30 mg
Fiber: 4 g
Exchange Approx.:
1 Fruit, 1 Fat, 1 Carb./ Sugar

*Vanilla extract contains a trace amount of sugar. You can substitute sugar-free organic extract if you prefer.

# Nonfat Ice Cream or Smoothie Base

**Serves 8**

¼ cup nonfat milk powder
1 cup skim milk
1 tablespoon lemon juice
2 tablespoons Splenda
    granular

**NUTRITIONAL ANALYSIS**
(per serving):

Calories: 20
Protein: 2 g
Carbohydrate: 3 g
Fat: trace
Sat. Fat: trace
Cholesterol: 1 mg
Sodium: 27 mg
Fiber: trace
Exchange Approx.:
½ Carb./Sugar, ½ Skim
Milk

1. Place all the ingredients in the blender and mix until well blended. Store in a covered container in the refrigerator until the expiration date shown on the milk carton.

# Mock Pumpkin Custard

1. Preheat oven to 375°F. Process all the ingredients in a food processor until puréed. Pour into a baking dish treated with nonstick spray. Bake for 30 minutes.

**Serves 8**

1¾ cup cooked pinto beans, drained
1½ cup skim milk
⅜ cup nonfat dry milk
2 eggs
¼ teaspoon sea salt
⅛ cup Splenda granular
1 teaspoon honey
1¼ teaspoon ground cinnamon
½ teaspoon ground cloves
⅛ teaspoon ground ginger

**NUTRITIONAL ANALYSIS**
(per serving):

Calories: 103
Protein: 7 g
Carbohydrate: 15 g
Fat: 2 g
Sat. Fat: 1 g
Cholesterol: 54 mg
Sodium: 60 mg
Fiber: 3 g
Exchange Approx.:
1½ Breads, ½ Fat

# Strawberry-Banana Sherbet

**Serves 4**

1⅓ cup strawberry halves
2 tablespoons Splenda
  granular
1 ripe (but not overly ripe)
  banana, mashed
1 tablespoon frozen orange
  juice concentrate
2 tablespoons water
1 tablespoon lemon juice
1 cup 1% milk
2 tablespoons nonfat milk
  powder

---

**NUTRITIONAL ANALYSIS**

(per serving):

Calories: 81
Protein: 3 g
Carbohydrate: 16 g
Fat: 1 g
Sat. Fat: trace
Cholesterol: 3 mg
Sodium: 44 mg
Fiber: 2 g
Exchange Approx.:
½ Skim Milk, ½ Fruit,
½ Carb.

1. Sprinkle the Splenda granular over the strawberries. Mash the strawberries with a fork, and allow a little time for the Splenda granular to dissolve and draw the juice out of the strawberries, then combine all the ingredients in a blender or food processor and process to desired consistency. (Some people prefer chunks of fruit; others like a smoother sherbet.)

2. Pour the mixture into an ice-cream maker and freeze according to manufacturer's directions, or pour the mixture into ice cube trays or a covered container and freeze overnight.

*TIP: Although you could use 1 cup of the Whipped Milk Base (see page 206) in this recipe in place of the Splenda granular and milk, the Splenda granular helps draw the juice from the strawberries, so it enhances the flavor.*

# Bananas Foster

Combine all the ingredients except the yogurt in a nonstick skillet, bring to a boil, and cook until the bananas are tender. Put 3 ounces of nonfat frozen vanilla yogurt in each dessert bowl or stemmed glass, and spoon the heated banana sauce over the top.

## Know Your Ingredients

Overripe bananas are higher in sugar and therefore can adversely affect your blood glucose levels. You can freeze bananas in the skins until ready to use. Doing so makes them perfect additions for fruit smoothies or fruit cups. Remove them from the freezer and run a little water over the peel to remove any frost. Peel them using a paring knife and slice according to the recipe directions. Frozen bananas can be added directly to smoothie and other recipes.

**Serves 4**

4 bananas, sliced
¼ cup unsweetened apple
  juice concentrate
Grated zest of 1 orange
¼ cup fresh orange juice
  (freshly squeezed)
1 tablespoon ground
  cinnamon
12 ounces lowfat no-sugar
  added frozen vanilla yogurt

**NUTRITIONAL ANALYSIS**
(per serving):

Calories: 216
Protein: 4 g
Carbohydrate: 48 g
Fat: 2 g
Sat. Fat: 1 g
Cholesterol: 4 mg
Sodium: 66 mg
Fiber: 4 g
Exchange Approx.:
2½ Fruits, 1 Skim Milk

# Almond Biscotti

**Yields 42 cookies**
**Serving size: 1 cookie**

1 cup Splenda granular
½ cup unsalted butter
1 tablespoon grated orange
    peel
2 eggs
3½ cups all-purpose flour
1 teaspoon baking powder
½ teaspoon sea salt
⅓ cup ground almonds

**NUTRITIONAL ANALYSIS**
(per serving):

Calories: 70
Protein: 2 g
Carbohydrate: 9 g
Fat: 3 g
Sat. Fat: 2 g
Cholesterol: 16 mg
Sodium: 38 mg
Fiber: trace
Exchange Approx.:
½ Fat, ½ Bread/Starch

1. Preheat oven to 350°F. Beat the Splenda granular, butter, orange peel, and eggs in a small bowl. Mix together the flour, baking powder, and salt in a large bowl, and stir in the egg mixture and almonds. Shape half of the dough at a time into a rectangle 10" × 3" and place on an ungreased baking sheet. Bake about 20 minutes or until an inserted toothpick comes out clean.

2. Cool on the baking sheet for 15 minutes. Cut into ½-inch slices, and place cut-side down on baking sheet. Bake for another 15 minutes, or until crisp and light brown. Cool on a wire rack.

# Beanberry Blast

Process all the ingredients, except the ice cubes, in a blender until smooth. Add the ice cubes and blend until smooth. (If frozen straw-berries are used, omit the ice cubes and thin with water, if necessary.) You can also prepare this the night before, mixing all of the ingredients except the ice. Add the ice cubes in the morning and process for an instant breakfast.

**Serves 4**

1 (15-ounce) can navy beans
   or Great Northern beans,
   drained and rinsed
1½ cups orange juice
2 cups sliced strawberries
1 tablespoon honey
1½ teaspoons ground
   cinnamon
⅛ teaspoon ground nutmeg
6–8 ice cubes

---

**NUTRITIONAL ANALYSIS**
(per serving):

Calories: 207
Protein: 1 g
Carbohydrate: 43 g
Fat: 1 g
Sat. Fat: trace
Cholesterol: 0 mg
Sodium: 245 mg
Fiber: 2 g
Exchange Approx.:
1½ Fruits, 1½ Breads

# Apple Cookies with a Kick

**Yields 24 cookies**
**Serving size: 1 cookie**

1 tablespoon ground flaxseed
¼ cup water
1 teaspoon honey
⅛ cup Splenda granular
¾ cup cooked pinto beans, drained
⅓ cup unsweetened applesauce
2 teaspoons baking powder
⅛ teaspoon sea salt
1 teaspoon ground cinnamon
½ teaspoon ground nutmeg
¼ teaspoon ground cloves
¼ teaspoon ground allspice
1 cup white flour
½ cup whole wheat flour
1 medium-sized golden delicious apple
1 cup sunflower seeds—dried, kernels (not roasted; unsalted)

1. Preheat oven to 350°F. Put the flaxseed and water in a microwave-safe container; microwave on high for 15 seconds or until the mixture thickens and has the consistency of egg whites. Add the flaxseed mixture, Splenda granular, honey, beans, and applesauce to a mixing bowl and mix well.

2. Sift the dry ingredients together, then fold into the bean mixture. (Do not overmix; this will cause the cookies to become tough.)

3. Peel and chop the apple and fold it and the sunflower seeds into the batter. Drop by teaspoonful onto a baking sheet treated with non-stick spray. Bake for 12 to 18 minutes.

## Creative Substitutions

Adding nuts and, of all things, beans to dessert recipes increases the amount of protein and fiber. Just because it's dessert doesn't mean it has to be all empty calories.

**NUTRITIONAL ANALYSIS**
(per serving):

Calories: 87
Protein: 3 g
Carbohydrate: 13 g
Fat: 3 g
Sat. Fat: trace
Cholesterol: 0 mg
Sodium: 52 mg
Fiber: 2 g
Exchange Approx.:
1 Fruit

# Lemon Curd

1. In a microwave-safe bowl, whip the eggs until fluffy. Gradually add the Splenda granular, salt, and lemon juice, beating well. Add the butter. Microwave on high for 20 seconds to melt the butter; stir well. Rotate the bowl and microwave at 80 percent power for 1 minute.

2. Whip the lemon fluff, then microwave at 80 percent power for 20 seconds; whip again, rotate bowl, and repeat process 2 (or so) more times, whipping after each time it is microwaved. The mixture should coat the back of a spoon, and will thicken more as it cools.

*TIP: Pour through a fine strainer to remove any cooked egg solids that didn't get blended into the mixture.*

## Juicy Gelatine

It's easy to make fruit juice gelatin. Add 1 tablespoon of unsweetened gelatine powder to ½ cup sugar free fruit juice. Allow to soften, then microwave on high for 30 seconds. Whisk to dissolve the gelatine, then stir in another 1 cup of fruit juice. (Kiwi fruit, mangoes, papaya, and pineapple juices won't work because they contain an enzyme that prevents gelling.) Refrigerate until set. Exchange Approximations will depend on the type of fruit juice you use and the size of the servings.

**Yields 1⅛ cup**
**Serving size: 1 tbs.**

2 eggs
¼ cup Splenda granular
⅛ teaspoon sea salt
¼ cup lemon juice
3 tablespoons butter

**NUTRITIONAL ANALYSIS**
(per serving):

Calories: 27
Protein: 1 g
Carbohydrate: 1 g
Fat: 2 g
Sat. Fat: 1 g
Cholesterol: 29 mg
Sodium: 40 mg
Fiber: trace
Exchange Approx.:
½ Fat, ½ Misc. Carb.

# Pineapple Upside-Down Cake

**Serves 8**

1 tablespoon honey
1 (8¼-ounce) can unsweetened, crushed pineapple in juice, (drained, juice reserved)
1 envelope KNOX Unflavored Gelatine
2 eggs
1 egg white
¾ cup Splenda granular
1 teaspoon vanilla*
¾ cup all-purpose flour
1 teaspoon baking powder
¼ teaspoon salt

**NUTRITIONAL ANALYSIS**
(per serving):

Calories: 94
Protein: 4 g
Carbohydrate: 16 g
Fat: 1 g
Sat. Fat: trace
Cholesterol: 53 g
Sodium: 154 g
Fiber: 1 mg
Exchange Approx.:
1 Bread, 1 Fruit

*Vanilla extract contains a trace amount of sugar. You can substitute sugar-free organic extract if you prefer.

1. Preheat oven to 375°F. Line a 9" × 1½" round baking pan with waxed paper and spray with nonstick cooking spray. Sprinkle the honey on the waxed paper. Spread the crushed pineapple evenly in the bottom of the pan and sprinkle the gelatine over the top.

2. In a large bowl, beat the eggs and egg white until very thick. Gradually beat in the Splenda granular. Add enough water to the reserved pineapple juice to measure ⅓ cup; beat it into the egg mixture along with the vanilla.

3. In a separate bowl, mix together the flour, baking powder, and salt; gradually add it to the egg mixture, beating until the batter is smooth. Pour into pan. Bake about 25 to 30 minutes, or until an inserted toothpick comes out clean. Immediately loosen the cake from the edge of pan with a knife and invert the pan on a plate. Carefully remove the waxed paper and slice into 8 pieces.

# Whole-Grain Maple-Walnut Bread Pudding

1. Preheat oven to 350°F. Put the first 7 ingredients in a food processor or blender and process until mixed. Tear the crustless bread into pieces and place in a mixing bowl. Pour the blended milk mixture over the bread, add the chopped walnuts, and toss to mix.

2. Pour the mixture into a nonstick spray–treated nonstick cake pan. Bake for 20 minutes (or until the egg is set). Cut into 8 pie-shaped wedges. Serve warm or chilled.

**Serves 8**

1 cup skim milk
⅜ cup dry nonfat milk powder
2 teaspoons unsalted butter
2 eggs
1 teaspoon vanilla*
3 tablespoons sugar-free maple syrup
1 tablespoon Splenda granular
4 ounces multigrain bread, crusts removed
¼ cup chopped walnuts
Pinch of sea salt (optional)

**NUTRITIONAL ANALYSIS**
(per serving):

Calories: 120
Protein: 7 g
Carbohydrate: 12 g
Fat: 5 g
Sat. Fat: 1 g
Cholesterol: 57 mg
Sodium: 156 mg
Fiber: 1 g
Exchange Approx.:
1 Starch, 1 Fat, ½ Misc. Carb.

*Vanilla extract contains a trace amount of sugar. You can substitute sugar-free organic extract if you prefer.*

# Individual Apple-Blackberry Charlottes

**Serves 6**

6 Golden Delicious apples, peeled and sliced
3 tablespoons seedless blackberry jam or preserves (fruit-only, no sugar added)
1 tablespoon unsalted butter, at room temperature
12 slices bread, crusts removed
⅛ cup (2 tablespoons) Mock Cream (see page 20)
1 egg
1 teaspoon vanilla**
1 tablespoon Splenda granular

**NUTRITIONAL ANALYSIS**
(per serving):

Calories: 170
Protein: 2 g
Carbohydrate: 34 g
Fat: 4 g
Sat. Fat: 2 g
Cholesterol: 37 mg
Sodium: 80 mg
Fiber: 4 g*
Exchange Approx.:
½ Fat, 1 Bread/Starch, 1 Fruit (*even higher if you use whole-grain bread)

**Vanilla extract contains a trace amount of sugar. You can substitute sugar-free organic extract if you prefer.*

1. Preheat oven to 350°F. Place the apples in a covered microwave-safe bowl and microwave on high until tender, about 5 minutes. Stir in the blackberry jam until the apples are well coated.

2. Prepare a 6-capacity, nonstick muffin tin (the kind used to make larger muffins) by spraying the bottom of each section with non-stick spray and coating the inside of each section with ½ teaspoon of the unsalted butter. Trim the bread so it's the same height as the depth of your muffin tin. Cut each slice into 3 strips.

3. In a small bowl, beat together the Mock Cream, egg, and vanilla. Dip each bread strip in the Mock Cream mixture. (Do not soak the bread in the mixture; you only want each strip lightly coated.) Leaving the bottom open, line the sides of each of the jumbo muffin-tin cups with 6 overlapping pieces of bread, pressing the bread against the butter-coated sides as you go.

4. Divide the apple mixture into each muffin tin section, ladling it in the center of the bread slices. Place the tins in the oven, and bake until the bread is golden brown on the outside, about 20 minutes.

5. Transfer the muffin pan to a wire rack to cool for 10 minutes. Unmold the charlottes by inverting onto a baking sheet or cutting board, then transfer each muffin to a dessert plate.

# Snacks and Drinks

## chapter thirteen

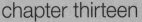
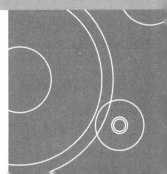

# Chocolate Candy Substitute

**Yields 15–20 pieces**

1 tablespoon unsweetened
   cocoa
1 tablespoon Splenda granular
¾ cup fresh pineapple chunks
1–3 teaspoons nonfat dry milk
   (optional)

**NUTRITIONAL ANALYSIS**
(per serving):

Calories: 6
Protein: trace
Carbohydrate: 1 g
Fat: trace
Sat. Fat: trace
Cholesterol: trace
Sodium: 2
Fiber: trace
Exchange Approx.:
(for entire recipe,
without dry milk):
1 Fruit, 1 Carb./Sugar,
1 Free Drink

1. In a small bowl, mix the cocoa and Splenda granular. Place waxed paper on a baking sheet. Dip each piece of pineapple in the cocoa-Splenda granular mixture. (The choice on whether to coat only 1 side of the pineapple or all sides depends on whether or not you prefer a "dark, bittersweet chocolate" taste or a milder one. Add the dry milk powder to the mixture if you prefer a "milk chocolate" flavor.) Place each piece of pineapple on the waxed paper–covered baking sheet. Place the baking sheet in the freezer for several hours.

2. Once the pineapple is frozen, layer the pineapple "candies" on waxed paper in an airtight freezer container. Place a piece of aluminum foil over the top layer before you put on the lid, to prevent freezer burn.

*TIP: The Exchange Approximations given for this recipe is for the entire amount; however, it's intended to be used as a way to curb a candy craving. (You grab a frozen chunk from the freezer and eat it like candy.) Discuss this recipe with your dietitian to see how you can fit it into your meal plan.*

# Honey Raisin Bars

1. Preheat oven to 350°F. Sift the flour, soda, salt, and cinnamon together into a bowl and stir in the oatmeal.

2. In another bowl, mix the slightly beaten egg whites with the oil, honey, milk, vanilla, and raisins. Add the flour mixture to liquid ingredients. Drop by teaspoon onto cookie sheets treated with nonstick spray. Bake for 12 to 15 minutes. (Longer baking time will result in crispier cookies.) Cool on a baking rack.

3. For cookie bars, spread the mixture in an even layer on a piece of parchment paper placed on the cookie sheet; bake for 15 to 18 minutes. Cool slightly, then use a sharp knife or pizza cutter to slice into 18 equal pieces (6 down, 3 across).

*TIP: If you like chewier cookies or need to cut the fat in your diet, you can substitute applesauce, plums, prunes, or mashed banana for the sunflower oil.*

**Yields 18 bars**

½ cup unbleached all-purpose flour
¼ teaspoon baking soda
⅛ teaspoon sea salt
¼ teaspoon cinnamon
¾ cup quick-cooking oatmeal
1 egg white, slightly beaten
2½ tablespoons sunflower oil
¼ cup honey
¼ cup skim milk
½ teaspoon vanilla*
½ cup golden raisins

**NUTRITIONAL ANALYSIS**
(per serving):

Calories: 71
Protein: 1 g
Carbohydrate: 12 g
Fat: 2 g
Sat. Fat: trace
Cholesterol: trace
Sodium: 39 mg
Fiber: 1 g
Exchange Approx.: ½ Bread, ½ Misc. Carb.

*Vanilla extract contains a trace amount of sugar. You can substitute sugar-free organic extract if you prefer.*

# No-Bake Chocolate–Peanut Butter Oatmeal Cookies

**Serves 12**

2 tablespoons butter
¼ cup unsweetened cocoa
½ cup Splenda granular
¼ cup Mock Cream (see page 20)
Dash of sea salt
1 teaspoon vanilla*
1 tablespoon peanut butter
1½ cups oatmeal

---

**NUTRITIONAL ANALYSIS**
(per serving):

Calories: 78
Protein: 3 g
Carbohydrate: 9 g
Fat: 3 g
Sat. Fat: 2 g
Cholesterol: 5 mg
Sodium: 50 mg
Fiber: 2 g
Exchange Approx.:
½ Fat, 1 Bread

*Vanilla extract contains a trace amount of sugar. You can substitute sugar-free organic extract if you prefer.*

1. Add the butter to a deep, microwave-safe bowl and microwave on high for 20 to 30 seconds, or until the butter is melted. Add the cocoa and stir to blend. Stir in the Splenda granular, Mock Cream, and salt. Microwave on high for 1 minute, 10 seconds to bring to a full boil. (Should you need to microwave the batter some more, do so in 10-second increments. You want a full boil, but because it will continue to cook for a while once it's removed from the microwave, heating it too long can cause the mixture to scorch.)

2. Add the vanilla and peanut butter and stir until mixed. Fold in the oatmeal. Drop by tablespoonful on waxed paper and allow to cool.

## Easy Graham Cracker Goodies

A little of this rich peanut butter and cream cheese goes a long way. To make 4 treats, mix 1 teaspoon peanut butter, 1 teaspoon cream cheese, and 2 teaspoons Splenda granular until well blended. Divide between 6 whole graham crackers. Spread an equal amount of the icing on top of each graham cracker. Allow 3 open-faced squares per serving. The Analysis is: Calories: 102; Protein: 2 g; Carbohydrate: 17 g; Fat: 3 g; Sat. Fat: 1 g; Cholesterol: 1 mg; Sodium: 137 mg; Fiber: 1 g; PCF Ratio: 8-63-29. Exchange Approximations: 1 Bread, 1 Fat.

# Tortilla Chips

Preheat oven to 400°F. Spray both sides of the tortilla with olive oil. Season lightly with sea salt or any season blend. Bake the tortilla on a cookie sheet until crisp and beginning to brown, about 2 to 5 minutes, depending on the thickness of the tortilla. Break the tortilla into large pieces.

*TIP: When you buy the tortillas, look for a brand made with only cornmeal, water, and lime juice. Nutritional Analysis and Exchange Approximations will depend on the brand of tortillas and the amount of oil you use.*

**Serves 1**

1 nonfat corn tortilla
Olive oil
Sea salt to taste (optional)
Seasoning blend of your
    choice, to taste

**NUTRITIONAL ANALYSIS**
(per serving):

Exchange Approx.:
1 Carb./Starch, ½ Fat

# Black Olive Mock Caviar

**Yields 1¼ cups**
**Serving size: 1 tbs.**

1 (5¾-ounce) can chopped
  black olives
1 (4-ounce) can chopped
  green chili peppers
1 cup diced fresh or canned
  (no salt added) tomato
2 tablespoons chopped green
  onions
1 clove garlic, minced
1 tablespoon extra-virgin
  olive oil
1 teaspoon red wine vinegar
Pinch of Splenda granular
½ teaspoon freshly ground
  black pepper

**NUTRITIONAL ANALYSIS**
(per serving):

Calories: 19
Protein: trace
Carbohydrate: 1 g
Fat: 2 g
Sat. Fat: trace
Cholesterol: 0 mg
Sodium: 72 mg
Fiber: trace
Exchange Approx.:
1 Free Condiment or
½ Fat

In a medium-sized mixing bowl, mix together all the ingredients. Cover, and chill overnight. Serve cold or at room temperature.

# Snack Mix

1. Preheat oven to 300°F. In a large bowl, combine the cereals, pretzels, and peanuts. In another bowl, combine the butter, oil, Worcestershire, garlic powder, and Tabasco (if using).

2. Pour over the cereal mixture and toss to coat evenly. Spread the mixture on a large baking sheet and bake for 30 to 40 minutes, stirring every 10 minutes, until crisp and dry. Cool and store in an airtight container. Serve at room temperature.

*TIP: The Nutritional Analysis will depend on the type of fat and cereals used in the recipe, most notably regarding the PCF Ratio.*

## Microwave Popcorn—from Scratch

To make "air-popped" popcorn in the microwave, add 1 cup of popcorn to a small brown paper bag. Fold down the top. Spray the bag with water (or wet your hand and tap water on each side and the bottom of the bag). Microwave on high for 3 minutes, or use the popcorn setting if your microwave has it.

**Serves 16**
**Serving Size: ½ cup**

6 cups mixed cereal (such as a mixture of unsweetened bran, oat, rice, and wheat cereals)
1 cup mini bow-knot pretzels
⅔ cup dry-roasted peanuts
⅛ cup (2 tablespoons) butter, melted
⅛ cup (2 tablespoons) olive, canola, or peanut oil
1 tablespoon Worcestershire sauce (see recipe for Homemade on page 17)
¼ teaspoon garlic powder
Tabasco sauce or other liquid hot pepper sauce to taste (optional)

**NUTRITIONAL ANALYSIS**
(per serving, on average):

Calories: 125
Protein: 3 g
Carbohydrate 16 g
Total Fat: variable
Cholesterol: 4 mg
Sodium: 201 mg
Fiber: 2 g
Exchange Approx.:
1 Carb./Starch, 1 Fat

# Asian Popcorn

**Serves 1**

4 cups air-popped popcorn
1 teaspoon Bragg's Liquid
    Aminos or low-sodium soy
    sauce
2 teaspoons fresh lemon juice
1 teaspoon five-spice powder
¼ teaspoon ground coriander
¼ teaspoon garlic powder

**NUTRITIONAL ANALYSIS**
(per serving):

Calories: 129
Protein: 5 g
Carbohydrate 26 g
Total Fat: 1 g
Sat. Fat: trace
Cholesterol: 0 mg
Sodium: 221 mg
Fiber: 5 g
Exchange Approx.:
1 Carb./Starch, 1 Free
Condiment

1. Preheat oven to 250°F. Spread the popcorn on a nonstick cookie sheet and lightly coat with nonstick or butter-flavored cooking spray.

2. Mix together all the remaining ingredients. Drizzle the mixture over the popcorn and lightly toss to coat evenly. Bake for 5 minutes, toss the popcorn and rotate the pan, and then bake for an additional 5 minutes. Serve warm.

## Keeping Snacks in Stock

Because there are no oils to go rancid, air-popped popcorn will keep for weeks if you store it in an airtight container. Pop up a large batch and keep some on hand for later. Then, depending on your mood, flavor it according to the suggestions in this section and you'll soon have a warm, healthy snack. Popcorn is a great snack. It's filling, it's good for you, and it's easy to prepare and keep on hand. Try different varieties so you don't get bored.

# Zucchini with Cheese Spread

Peel the zucchini and cut it into ¼-inch slices. Mix together the remaining ingredients except the green onion until well blended. Spread 1–2 teaspoons of the cream cheese mixture onto each slice of zucchini and place on a serving platter. Sprinkle with green onion, cover, and refrigerate for 1 hour or until firm.

## Simple Substitutions

Squash seeds are delicious when roasted, too. Serve them as snacks or as a garnish on soups or salads.

**Serves 8**

1 large green zucchini
⅓ cup softened fat-free cream cheese
¼ cup finely chopped red bell pepper
2 teaspoons dried parsley
¼ teaspoon onion powder
¼ teaspoon dried Italian seasoning
2 drops red pepper sauce
1 green onion, thinly sliced

---

**NUTRITIONAL ANALYSIS**
(per serving):

Calories: 38
Protein: 4 g
Carbohydrate: 4 g
Fat: trace
Sat. Fat: trace
Cholesterol: 2 mg
Sodium: 140 mg
Fiber: 2 g
Exchange Approx.:
1 Vegetable, ½ Fat

# Toasted Pumpkin Seeds

**Serves 8**

2 cups pumpkin seeds, scooped from a fresh pumpkin
Sea salt (optional)
1 tablespoons olive, peanut, or canola oil

**NUTRITIONAL ANALYSIS**
(per serving, without salt):

Calories: 202
Protein: 8 g
Carbohydrate: 6 g
Fat: 18 g
Sat. Fat: 3 g
Cholesterol: 0 mg
Sodium: 6 mg
Fiber: 1 g
Exchange Approx.:
1 Lean Meat, 3 Fats

1. Rinse the pumpkin seeds, removing all pulp and strings. Spread the seeds in a single layer on a large baking sheet and let them air-dry for at least 3 hours.

2. Preheat oven to 375°F. Drizzle the oil over the seeds and lightly sprinkle with salt, if using. (Alternative method would be to put dried pumpkin seeds in a plastic bag and add the oil. Seal the bag and toss to mix the seeds with the oil.) Toss, then spread them out in a single layer. Bake for 15 to 20 minutes, until lightly browned and toasted. Stir the seeds occasionally during the baking to allow for even browning. Remove the hulls to eat.

# Coffee-Spice Snack Cake

1. Preheat oven to 325°F. Pour 1 cup honey, coffee, and brandy into a bowl and mix well. Add the egg substitute, oil, and remaining honey, and beat until combined.

2. Sift together the flour, baking powder, baking soda, salt, and spices, and fold into the mixture. Pour the batter into a 9-inch-square baking dish treated with nonstick cooking spray. Bake for 50 to 60 minutes, or until an inserted toothpick comes out clean. Slice into 16 pieces.

**Serves 16**

1 cup honey
½ cup strong brewed coffee
1 tablespoon brandy
½ cup reduced-fat egg substitute
2 tablespoons olive oil
½ cup honey
2 cups all-purpose flour
1½ teaspoons baking powder
1½ teaspoons baking soda
½ teaspoon salt
½ teaspoon ground cinnamon
¼ teaspoon ground ginger
⅛ teaspoon ground nutmeg
⅛ teaspoon ground cloves

**NUTRITIONAL ANALYSIS**
(per serving):

Calories: 170
Protein: 2 g
Carbohydrate: 43 g
Fat: trace
Sat. Fat: trace
Cholesterol: 0 mg
Sodium: 243 mg
Fiber: 1 g
Exchange Approx.: 2 Carbs./Starches, ½ Fat

# Creamy Fruit Cup

**Serves 1**

4 ounces (half of a small
   container) nonfat plain
   yogurt
1 tablespoon unsweetened
   applesauce
1 teaspoon lemon juice
½ cup cubed fresh or frozen
   cantaloupe
¼ cup cubed or sliced apple
6 seedless red or green
   grapes
Lemon zest (optional)

**NUTRITIONAL ANALYSIS**
(per serving, without additional applesauce or jelly):

Calories: 129
Protein: 7 g
Carbohydrate: 26 g
Fat: 1 g
Sat. Fat: trace
Cholesterol: 0 mg
Sodium: 89 mg
Fiber: 2 g
Exchange Approx.:
½ Skim Milk, 1½ Fruits

1. Mix together the yogurt, applesauce, and lemon juice; drizzle over the mixed fruit. (If you prefer a sweeter dressing, you can add another tablespoon of applesauce or blend in 2 teaspoons of sugar-free apple jelly without increasing the number of Fruit Exchanges; adjust the calorie count accordingly.) For a more zesty (and attractive!) dish, sprinkle lemon zest over the top of the dressing.

*TIP: Prepare the Creamy Fruit Cup for your lunchbox! If you do, keep the dressing and fruits in separate containers until you're ready to serve. To keep the lemon zest moist, you can mix it in with the dressing.*

## Just Juice?

Fruit and fruit juice provide healthy nutrients, and, in most cases, fiber, too. That's the good news. The downside is they also convert quickly to glucose. For that reason, many people can only consume them as part of a meal, rather than alone as a snack.

# Sparkling Fruited Iced Tea

In a pitcher, mix together the tea, orange juice, and lemon juice. In tall, iced-tea glasses (16- to 20-ounce size), place 4 or 5 ice cubes. Pour the tea and juice mixture over the ice, then evenly divide the ginger ale between the glasses. Add carbonated water to finish filling the glasses. Stir to mix and serve.

**Serves 4**

3 cups decaffeinated tea
1 cup unsweetened orange juice
4 teaspoons fresh lemon juice
1 (12-ounce) can carbonated ginger ale
Seltzer water, club soda, or other unsweetened carbonated water

---

**NUTRITIONAL ANALYSIS**
(per serving):

Calories: 31
Protein: trace
Carbohydrate: 7 g
Fat: trace
Sat. Fat: trace
Cholesterol: 0 mg
Sodium: 46 mg
Fiber: trace
Exchange Approx.:
1 Fruit

# Minted Lemon Tea

**Serves 4**

4 cups boiling water
4 tea bags
1 teaspoon chopped fresh
    mint or ¼ teaspoon dried
    mint flakes
Juice of 1 lemon (about 3–4
    teaspoons)
¼ cup honey

In a ceramic or glass container, pour the boiling water over the tea bags and mint. Cover and allow to steep for 5 minutes. Add the lemon juice and honey. Stir until the honey is dissolved. Strain the mixture and divide between 4 mugs.

**NUTRITIONAL ANALYSIS**
(per serving):

Calories: 67
Protein: trace
Carbohydrate: 18 g
Fat: 0 g
Sat. Fat: 0 g
Cholesterol: 0 mg
Sodium: 8 mg
Fiber: trace
Exchange Approx.:
1 Carb./Sugar

# Iced Ginger-Orange Green Tea

In medium saucepan, bring the water to boil. In a ceramic container, pour the boiling water over the ginger and orange peel. Add tea bags; cover, and steep for 5 minutes. Remove the tea bags, ginger, and orange peel. Add the orange juice to the tea blend, and stir. Put ice cubes in 4 glasses, pour orange juice–tea blend over the ice, and serve.

## Monitor Your Exchanges

If you add additional sweetener to any of the tea recipes, be sure to include that Exchange List choice as well, if applicable.

**Serves 4**

2 cups water
1 tablespoon coarsely
   chopped crystallized ginger
2 (1-inch) pieces orange zest
4 green tea bags
2 cups orange juice, chilled

**NUTRITIONAL ANALYSIS**
(per serving):

Calories: 62
Protein: 1 g
Carbohydrate: 15 g
Fat: trace
Sat. Fat: trace
Cholesterol: 0 mg
Sodium: 9 mg
Fiber: trace
Exchange Approx.:
1 Fruit

# Hot Spiced Tea

**Serves 4**

2 tea bags
14 whole cloves
1 cinnamon stick
1 strip (about 3 inches) fresh
   orange zest
2 cups boiling water
¼ cup orange juice
1½ tablespoons lemon juice

**NUTRITIONAL ANALYSIS**
(per serving):

Calories: 8
Protein: trace
Carbohydrate: 2 g
Fat: trace
Sat. Fat.: 0 g
Cholesterol: 0 mg
Sodium: 3 mg
Fiber: 0 g
Exchange Approx.:
½ Free

Put the tea bags, spices, and orange peel in a ceramic or glass container and pour the boiling water over them; cover and allow to steep for 5 minutes. Strain the mixture. Stir in the orange and lemon juices; reheat if necessary. You can also chill it and serve over ice for a refreshing iced tea.

# Iced and Spiced Chai-Style Tea

In a medium saucepan, bring the milk just to boil. Stir in the remaining ingredients except for the carbonated water. Reduce heat to low and simmer, uncovered, for 3 minutes. Remove the tea bags and strain; chill. Serve over ice, adding an equal amount of the carbonated water to each serving.

*TIP: Alternative serving suggestion: This tea is also terrific when served warm in mugs; just replace the carbonated water with warm water.*

**Serves 4**

2 cups skim milk
¼ cup honey (optional)
½ teaspoon ground cinnamon
¼ teaspoon ground ginger
⅛ teaspoon allspice
4 tea bags
2 cups chilled, unflavored, unsweetened carbonated water

**NUTRITIONAL ANALYSIS**
(per serving):

Calories: 108
Protein: 4 g
Carbohydrate: 23 g
Fat: 1 g
Sat. Fat.: trace
Cholesterol: 0 mg
Sodium: 65 mg
Fiber: trace
Exchange Approx.:
1 Misc. Carb., ½ Skim Milk

# Spiced Chai-Style Creamer Mix

**Yields 15 teaspoons**
**Serving size: 1 tbs.**

½ cup nonfat dry milk
1½ teaspoons cinnamon
¼ teaspoon nutmeg
¼ teaspoon ground cloves
½ teaspoon ginger
¼ teaspoon allspice
¼ cup Splenda granular

**NUTRITIONAL ANALYSIS**
(per serving):

Calories: 65
Protein: 6 g
Carbohydrate: 10 g
Fat: trace
Sat. Fat: trace
Cholesterol: 3 mg
Sodium: 81 mg
Fiber: 1 g
Exchange Approx.:
1 Misc. Carb.

Combine all the ingredients in a lidded jar and shake to mix. Store in a cool, dry place. Because this recipe uses noninstant non-fat milk, it must be stirred into hot liquid. For iced tea, you can mix in the "creamer" using a blender.

# Tangy Limeade

1. Roll the limes on a cutting board using hard pressure to loosen the flesh and release the juice easily. Cut the limes in half and juice them, minus any seeds and the pith. Place the rinds in a non-corrosive metal or glass container, cover with the Splenda granular, and set aside.

2. Bring the water to boil and then pour it over the lime juice, rinds, and Splenda granular mixture. Allow the mixture to steep for 5 to 10 minutes, depending on your taste. (Two minutes is sufficient for an intense lime flavor; 10 minutes will have a hint of bitterness. If you prefer a sweeter limeade, omit the rinds and steep the mixture with the juice and pulp.)

3. If you're using the optional salt, add it now and stir thoroughly. Strain the warm liquid. Add ice cubes and stir until the ice is melted. Serve over additional ice cubes.

## Carbonated Limeade

To make a concentrate that can be stored in the refrigerator for up to 3 days, reduce the boiling water to 1 cup in the Limeade recipe. In a glass, combine 3 tablespoons of the concentrate with enough seltzer water or club soda to fill an 8- to 12-ounce glass. Remember that more carbonated water will produce a weaker-tasting beverage. Exchange Approximations: 1 Misc. Carb, ½ Fruit.

**Serves 8**

6 fresh limes
½ cup Splenda granular
2½ cups water
½ teaspoon salt (optional)
12 ice cubes (or 1½ cups cold water)

**NUTRITIONAL ANALYSIS**
(per serving, without salt):

Calories: 21
Protein: trace
Carbohydrate: 7 g
Fat: trace
Sat. Fat: trace
Cholesterol: 0 mg
Sodium: 137 mg
Fiber: trace
Exchange Approx.:
1 Misc. Carb.

# Frothy Orange Jewel

**Serves 1**

¼ cup fresh orange juice
1 cup skim milk
1½ teaspoon Splenda granular
½ teaspoon vanilla*
1–2 ice cubes (optional)

---

**NUTRITIONAL ANALYSIS**
(per serving):

Calories: 123
Protein: 9 g
Carbohydrate: 20 g
Fat: trace
Sat. Fat: trace
Cholesterol: 4 mg
Sodium: 128 mg
Fiber: trace
Exchange Approx.:
1 Fruit, 1 Skim Milk

*Vanilla extract contains a trace amount of sugar. You can substitute sugar-free organic extract if you prefer.

Combine all the ingredients in a blender and process until mixed. Serve in a frosted glass. If you don't have fresh orange juice on hand, you can substitute 1 tablespoon frozen orange juice concentrate and 3 tablespoons of water.

# Orange-Pineapple Froth

Combine all the ingredients in a blender container and process until mixed. Serve in a chilled glass.

**Serves 1**

1 tablespoon frozen orange juice concentrate
1 tablespoon frozen pineapple juice concentrate
1 cup skim milk
½ cup chilled water
½ teaspoon vanilla*

**NUTRITIONAL ANALYSIS**
(per serving):

Calories: 153
Protein: 9 g
Carbohydrate: 27 g
Fat: 1 g
Sat. Fat: trace
Cholesterol: 5 mg
Sodium: 129 mg
Fiber: trace
Exchange Approx.:
2 Fruits, 1 Skim Milk

*Vanilla extract contains a trace amount of sugar. You can substitute sugar-free organic extract if you prefer.*

# Party Time Minted Raspberry Lemonade

**Yields about 4 quarts**

1 cup raspberries
3 cups freshly squeezed lemon juice (12 to 15 lemons)
1½ cups Splenda granular
12 cups water
1 tablespoon finely chopped fresh mint (or 1 teaspoon dried mint)

---

**NUTRITIONAL ANALYSIS**
(per serving):

Calories: 24
Protein: trace
Carbohydrate: 7 g
Fat: trace
Sat. Fat: trace
Cholesterol: 0 mg
Sodium: 6 mg
Fiber: 1 g
Exchange Approx.:
½ Fruit, 1 Misc. Carb.

Mash the raspberries and press through a sieve to remove the seeds. Add the raspberries and other ingredients to a gallon container and stir until the Splenda granular is dissolved. Serve chilled or over ice.

## Bubbly Touch-of-Fruit-Taste Drink

Another soft drink option is to pour a cup of chilled, unsweetened club soda or seltzer over fresh or frozen fruit. The fruit imparts subtle flavor and sweetness to the beverage and when your drink is gone, you can eat the fruit for dessert. Nutritional Analysis depends on the chosen fruit, but for any choice, the Exchange Approximation is: ½ Fruit.

# Buttermilk Blush

Combine all the ingredients in a blender and process until mixed. Serve in a chilled glass.

**Serves 1**

½ cup chilled tomato juice or
   ½ cup chilled vegetable
   juice
½ cup cold buttermilk
½ teaspoon fresh lemon juice
Dash of Tabasco sauce
   (optional)

**NUTRITIONAL ANALYSIS**
(per serving):

Calories: 71
Protein: 5 g
Carbohydrate: 11 g
Fat: 1 g
Sat. Fat: 1 g
Cholesterol: 4 mg
Sodium: 141 mg
Fiber: 1 g
Exchange Approx.: ½
Skim Milk, 1 Vegetable

# Pineapple-Banana Blast

**Serves 1**

¼ frozen banana, sliced
1 tablespoon frozen pineapple juice concentrate
3 tablespoons water
½ cup buttermilk

Combine all the ingredients in a blender and process until mixed. Serve in a chilled glass.

**NUTRITIONAL ANALYSIS**
(per serving):

Calories: 109
Protein: 5 g
Carbohydrate: 21 g
Fat: 1 g
Sat. Fat: 1 g
Cholesterol: 4 mg
Sodium: 129 mg
Fiber: 1 g
Exchange Approx.:
1 Fruit, ½ Skim Milk

# Peachy Ginger Ale

1. Peel the peach and cut into 10 slices. Place 8 slices on a tray and set in the freezer. Put the remaining 2 slices of peach in a bowl and mash with a fork. Add the Splenda granular and mash it in with the peach; set aside.

2. In a microwave-safe container, mix the minced ginger with the water and microwave on high for 2 minutes. Cover the container and allow the mixture to steep for 5 minutes. Strain the ginger water (to remove the ginger) over the peach-Splenda granular mixture. Stir until the Splenda granular is completely dissolved.

3. Remove the peach slices from freezer and put 2 slices in each of 4 (12-ounce) glasses. Divide the ginger-peach mixture between the glasses. Pour the unsweetened carbonated water over the frozen fruit, and stir. Serve with an iced-tea spoon, and enjoy the fruit for dessert.

## Unbelievable Fact

There are 9 teaspoons of sugar in a 12-ounce can of regular soft drink. (Source: American Diabetes Association, *www.diabetes.org*)

**Serves 4**

1 large peach
⅛ cup Splenda granular
2 teaspoons minced fresh ginger
⅛ cup water
Unsweetened club soda, seltzer water, or carbonated water

**NUTRITIONAL ANALYSIS**
(per serving):

Calories: 23
Protein: trace
Carbohydrate: 6 g
Fat: trace
Sat. Fat: trace
Cholesterol: 0 mg
Sodium: 1 mg
Fiber: 1 g
Exchange Approx.:
½ Fruit, ½ Misc. Carb.

# Fruit Frenzy Sparkler Concentrate

**Serves 8**

1 cup peeled, seeded, and
  chopped peach or papaya
1 cup peeled, cubed fresh
  pineapple
1 teaspoon peeled, grated
  fresh ginger
1 cup orange juice
1 cup frozen banana slices
Unsweetened club
  soda, seltzer water, or
  carbonated water

Place all the ingredients in a food processor and process until smooth. To serve, pour ½ cup of the concentrate over ice in a 12- to 16-ounce glass. Complete filling the glass with carbonated water.

---

**NUTRITIONAL ANALYSIS**
(per serving):

Calories: 53
Protein: 1 g
Carbohydrate: 13 g
Fat: trace
Sat. Fat: trace
Cholesterol: 0 mg
Sodium: 1 mg
Fiber: 1 g
Exchange Approx.:
1 Fruit

# Strawberry Cooler

In a large tumbler, combine ½ cup frozen strawberries. Pour ¼ cup apple juice over the strawberries, and finish filling the glass with the sparkling water. Stir, and serve with an iced-tea spoon; eat the fruit at the end of your meal for dessert.

**Serves 1**

½ cup frozen strawberries
¼ cup apple juice
Sparkling water

---

**NUTRITIONAL ANALYSIS**
(per serving):

Calories: 52
Protein: 1 g
Carbohydrate: 13 g
Fat: trace
Sat. Fat: trace
Cholesterol: 0 mg
Sodium: 3 mg
Fiber: 2 g
Exchange Approx.:
1 Fruit

# Nectarine Cocktail

**Serves 4**

2 cups buttermilk
2 large, chilled nectarines
1 teaspoon Splenda granular
1 teaspoon sugar-free maple-
flavored syrup

## NUTRITIONAL ANALYSIS
(per serving):

Calories: 103
Protein: 5 g
Carbohydrate: 19 g
Fat: 2 g
Sat. Fat: 1 g
Cholesterol: 4 mg
Sodium: 129 mg
Fiber: 2 g
Exchange Approx.:
1 Fruit, ½ Skim Milk

Combine 2 cups buttermilk, 2 large, chilled nectarines, peeled and cut into pieces, Splenda granular, and 1 teaspoon sugar-free maple-flavored syrup in a blender and process until the nectarines are puréed. Serve in a chilled glass.

# Jam and Jelly
# Soft Drink Syrup

Microwave 2 teaspoons sugar-free jam or jelly and 1 tablespoon water on high for 30 seconds to 1 minute; stir. Put ice cubes in a 12- to 16-ounce glass. Pour the "syrup" over the ice, and fill the glass with carbonated water. The Nutritional Analysis depends on the fruit you choose.

**Serves 1**

2 teaspoons sugar-free jam
   or jelly
1 tablespoon water
Ice cubes
Carbonated water
Your choice of fruit

**NUTRITIONAL ANALYSIS**
(per serving):

Exchange Approx.:
1 Free

# Online Sources for Gourmet Ingredients and Equipment

## appendix A

The quality of the foods you prepare is based on the quality of the ingredients you use. That's elementary. The equipment you use can make a difference, too. Even if you don't have a gourmet grocery or cooking supply store nearby, you don't have to forego using sherry vinegar or chestnuts or truffle oil or any other out-of-the-ordinary ingredient or product you've been wanting to try. Chances are you can order it online through one of these sites:

### Chef's Catalog
*www.chefscatalog.com*

### Christine and Rob's
"America's Gourmet Breakfast Company"
*www.christineandrobs.com*

### Country Life Natural Foods
*www.clnf.org*

### Earthy Delights
*www.earthy.com*

### Florentyna's Fresh Pasta Factory
*www.florentynaspasta.com*

### H&H Bagels
*www.hhbagels.com*

### Lobster Gram
*www.livelob.com*

### Kalyx.com
*www.kalyx.com*

### MexGrocer.com
*www.mexgrocer.com*

### Montana Organic Farms, Inc.
(Organic meats)
*www.mtorganicfarms.com*

**Organic Valley Family of Farms**
(Has Nutritional Analysis information online for
their meats)
*www.organicvalley.com*

**Russ & Daughters**
*www.russanddaughters.com*

**Seattle's Finest Exotic Meats**
*www.exoticmeats.com*

**Sur La Table**
*www.surlatable.com*

**Vermont Natural Meats**
*www.naturalmeat.com*

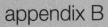

Living a No-Sugar Life

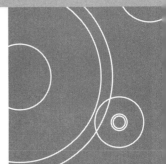

# Weights and Measures: Portion Control

You can't measure every morsel that passes your lips, but it's a good idea to measure most foods and beverages until you get a feel for portion sizes. It's a super-sized world out there, and most people are surprised to find that their idea of a single serving is actually two or three.

If you're into bells and whistles, there are food scales that are pre-programmed with nutritional information, as well as scales that will keep a running total of your daily food and nutrient intake for you. The only tools you really need, however, are a simple and inexpensive gram scale, dry and liquid measuring cups, and measuring spoons. Early on, it's a good idea to run everything that isn't premeasured through a scale, cup, or spoon first.

### Ballparking It

Get intimate with your food, or rather, your dishes. Have a favorite mug or bowl? Pay attention to how completely a serving of yogurt or soup fills it up. You'll soon find that it's second nature to guesstimate your portion sizes.

There will be times when you can't use your favorite cup. Pulling out a gram scale at your favorite restaurant is a little unrealistic. In these cases, it helps to have some rough equivalents for comparison.

Here are some typical serving sizes and some points of reference for estimating portion sizes:

- A cup of fruit or yogurt—a baseball, a clenched fist, or a small apple
- Three ounces of fish, meat, or poultry—a deck of cards, the palm of your hand, or a pocket pack of tissues
- One teaspoon butter or mayonnaise—a thimble, a thumb tip (top knuckle to tip), or the head of a toothbrush
- One ounce of cheese—your entire thumb, a tube of Chapstick, or an AA battery

Using your hands to estimate servings is probably the easiest method—you don't leave home without them. However, make sure you compare your hand amounts against food that has been measured out until you get a sense of how accurately you're estimating. Of course, if you have particularly large or small hands, you need to adjust for size.

Even for the more experienced portion predictor, it's a good idea to test your skills at least once a month and measure your guess at a serving size. It's easy to start overdoing it, and the little bits (and bites) add up. If your control has been off for no apparent reason, one of the first things to check is whether your serving sizes are on target.

### Eating Out

Restaurants are notorious for serving up heaping helpings well beyond a single serving size. To keep your intake under control, you can split an entrée, order off the appetizer menu, or simply eat half and take half home. In some restaurants, you may be able to order a child-size portion (but even some children's menu items may be larger than a single serving). Ask your server to serve condiments on the side so your food isn't swimming in sauce, and stay away from the bread basket, chips, or other complimentary snacks if you're fond of munching mindlessly.

When planning a meal out, don't set yourself up for failure. Choose a place that you know offers some food choices that will fit in to your meal plan. If you must meet at the local greasy spoon where lard is a food group, fill up on a healthy meal at home first. If you're on the road or in unfamiliar territory, don't be afraid to phone first or ask to see a menu at the door before committing to a restaurant choice. Ask questions about ingredients and preparation method. If you feel a need to explain why you won't be eating somewhere, tell the hostess you're on a special diet. Some establishments may offer to prepare a dish in an alternate way (e.g., steaming instead of frying it) that isn't on the regular menu to keep your patronage.

## When Temptation Strikes

You've had a delicious, yet healthy meal and are feeling pleased with yourself for turning down the bacon double cheeseburger that had been calling your name for broiled fish and steamed veggies. And then—the torture device rolls into view, a dessert cart laden with trays of your favorite cheesecake, hot fudge cake, and apple-caramel pie. You can feel your blood sugar rising just looking at it.

You can say "to hell with it!" and order the richest slice of cake on the cart; grin and bear it while your dining companion savors his slice of pie à la mode; or use the situation as an opportunity to practice moderation. You will not be struck by lightning if you indulge occasion-ally, provided your splurges are factored in to your overall meal plan. Split a small dessert with a friend, or ask for half now and half in a takeout bag. If the offerings are truly too rich for your blood, promise yourself a frozen yogurt or another favorite treat on your way home. Don't deny yourself—it's not an all-or-nothing game. Social occasions that are centered around eating, such as a birthday party, a holiday gathering, or a family reunion barbeque, offer a whole new set of chal-lenges. Well-meaning friends and relatives frequently feel the need to be the food police, asking with every pass of the plate, "Should you be eating that?" The best answer is simple: "Most people can eat just about anything you can, in moderation. I have a few books you can borrow that explain more if you're interested." Ideally, they'll take you up on your offer and learn a thing or two. If they don't, you've probably stopped them from pestering you, at least until Thanksgiving.

### Smart Snack Substitutes

Even though you can indulge occasionally, if you've made a regular habit of junk food, it's one you'll have to kick. Having many small healthy meals, or mini-snacks between meals, can help to keep you satisfied throughout the day.

Cut out the fatty fried snacks, sugary drinks and sodas, and sugar-crusted snack pies, and try some of these healthier snack choices instead, all with around 15 grams of carbs (one carb choice) or less:

- Air-popped popcorn (3 cups)
- Snack-size sugar-free Jell-O with Cool Whip
- Five whole-wheat crackers with peanut butter (1 tablespoon)
- Sugar-free pudding (½ cup)
- Two small tangerines
- Baked tortilla chips (15 to 20) and salsa

### Regaining Control After a Slip-up

If you haven't already, at one point in your life you will probably say "uh oh!" after splurging on something you shouldn't have. Ask yourself if there was a specific trigger for the slip-up, such as a particularly stress-ful day at work or going to a party hungry. If you can pinpoint a cause, think about how you can prevent it from happening next time, whether it be by adjusting your eating schedule or learning some stress management techniques.

It is not the end of the world if you screw up. If you're too busy kicking yourself, you'll miss any lesson you might gain from your mistake. There will undoubtedly be good times and bad. Strive to achieve balance in the emotional area as well as the physical one.

## Exercise: Getting Started

The first order of business with any exercise plan, especially if you're a dyed-in-the-wool couch potato, is to consult with your health care provider. If you have cardiac risk factors, she may want to perform a stress test to establish a safe level of exercise for you. Also, if you are diabetic, be sure to check with your physician about complications and how to avoid them.

### Start Slow

Your exercise routine can be as simple as a brisk nightly neighborhood walk. If you haven't been very active before now, start slowly and work your way up. Walk the dog or get out in the yard and rake. Take the stairs instead of the elevator. Park in the back of the lot and walk. Every little bit does, in fact, help.

As little as fifteen to thirty minutes of daily, heart-pumping exercise can make a big difference in your blood glucose control and your risk of developing diabetic complications. One of the easiest and least expensive ways of getting moving is to start a walking program. All you need is a good pair of well-fitting, supportive shoes and a direction to head in.

### Making Time

Everyone is busy. But considering what's at stake, making time for exercise needs to be a priority right now. Thirty minutes a day isn't much when you get right down to it. Cut one prime-time show out of your evening television viewing schedule. Get up a half-hour earlier each morning. Use half of your lunch hour for a brisk walk. You can find the time if you look hard enough for it.

You can also try combining exercise with something else already on your schedule. If you normally spend an hour on Saturday morning playing video games with your kids, take it out of virtual reality and play a real game of touch football or Frisbee outside. Get off the riding mower and cut the grass the old-fashioned way—with a manual push mower. Wake up early and walk your kids to school. Look for opportunities rather than excuses.

## Exercise Intensity

How hard you should be pushing yourself depends on your level of fitness and your health history. Your doctor can recommend an optimal heart rate target for working out based on these factors.

On average, most people should aim for a target heart rate zone of 50 to 75 percent of your maximum heart rate. Maximum heart rate is computed by subtracting your age from the number 220. So if you are 40, your maximum heart rate would be 180, and your target heart rate zone would be between 90 and 135 beats per minute.

You should wear a digital or analog watch with a second hand or function to check your heart rate during exercise. You can calculate heart rate by placing your fingers at your wrist or neck pulse point and counting the number of beats for fifteen seconds. Multiply that number by four to get your heart rate.

The number you get should be within your target zone. If it's too high, take your intensity down a few notches. If you're exercising below your target zone, pick things up. If you are new to exercise, you should aim for the lower (50 percent) range of your target heart rate. As you become more fit, you can work toward the 75 percent maximum.

## Everyone Can Exercise

Virtually everyone who has the capability to move can exercise to some degree. Even if you suffer from complications related to your diabetes or other health conditions, your doctor can recommend a level and form of exercise that is appropriate for you.

Chances are that you already work out without even knowing it. Things you have never considered "exercise," like washing the car or cleaning your house, are actually calorie-burning, heart-pumping ways to get fit. According to the U.S. Surgeon General, all of the following activities will burn about 150 calories a day (or 1,000 calories a week):

- Washing and waxing a car for 45 to 60 minutes
- Washing windows or floors for 45 to 60 minutes
- Gardening for 30 to 45 minutes
- Pushing a stroller 1.5 miles in 30 minutes
- Raking leaves for 30 minutes
- Walking 2 miles in 30 minutes (15 minutes per mile)
- Doing water aerobics for 30 minutes
- Bicycling 4 miles in 15 minutes
- Shoveling snow for 15 minutes
- Climbing steps for 15 minutes

### Disabled and Chronically Ill

For people with orthopedic conditions, joint pain, or musculoskeletal problems, low-impact exercise is usually the best bet. Swimming is a good low-impact form of resistance exercise. If you are in a wheelchair or unable to stand or stay on your feet for long periods of time without support, chair exercises may also be a good option. There are a number of chair exercise videotapes available for home workouts.

### Dealing with Obesity

If you are extremely overweight or obese, exercise is especially important, yet can present unique challenges. Comfort is an issue; certain exercises like jogging and high-impact aerobics may simply not be feasible. Weight lies heavy on the mind as well as the body, and it's possible you may not be feeling mentally or emotionally prepared to join group or team exercises.

Work on your own level. Don't try step aerobics just yet. Contact your local Y or community center to see if there's a plus-size exercise program available. And always check with your doctor before starting a new fitness routine. A referral to an exercise physiologist may be appropriate, particularly if you have other health problems.

It may be easier said than done, but don't feel self-conscious. If you feel uncomfortable amid all the spandex and ripped abs at the local health club, then don't torture yourself—find an environment that you feel at ease in. Try a walking program, either outside or at home on a treadmill. The impact-free environment of a pool is also a good place to start getting fit. Buddy up with a friend and motivate each other.

Exercise should make you feel good about yourself. Every step you take is a step toward a healthier you.

### Exercising for the Elderly
Staying active is particularly important as you grow older. Keep on track with an active lifestyle and strength-training exercises to retain muscle mass and insulin sensitivity. It's never too late to get moving. Talk to your doctor today about an appropriate exercise program that promotes strength, balance, flexibility, and endurance.

### Get Your Kids to Exercise, Too
Children are probably the least likely to need motivation to exercise. After all, most parents have a harder time keeping kids quiet than getting them moving. For overweight children or adolescents, and especially for those who are considered at risk for Type 2 Diabetes, exercise is absolutely imperative for all the reasons previously cited for adults— weight loss, improved awareness, and overall health and well-being. Teaching children from a young age that exercise is important can help to keep them healthy their entire lives.

## Staying Motivated
One of the biggest obstacles to staying on track for fitness is losing motivation. People who are just starting an exercise program can find themselves quickly tired of the same routine. Keeping exercise appealing and maintaining a good fitness perspective is key to long-term success.

If you had to watch the exact same episode of your favorite television show every day for the rest of your life, you'd probably be banging your head against the wall by the end of the week. You'd change the channel, pick up a book, or do anything you could to avoid something you once enjoyed. Yet many people starting on a fitness program feel compelled to follow the same routine, day after day after day, and consequently fall off the exercise wagon due to sheer boredom. Try these strategies for keeping your workouts interesting.

- Mix and match. Play racquetball with a friend one week and try water polo the next.
- Buddy up. Get a walking partner or an exercise buddy to keep you motivated (and vice versa).

- Join a team. Find a local softball league or aerobics group. Even when you aren't feeling much like exercising, your commitment to other team members may get you moving.
- Relocate. If you like to bike, walk, or jog, try a new route or locale.
- Go for the goal. Set new fitness targets for yourself.
- Reward yourself. When you reach a new goal, pat yourself on the back with a non-edible reward.
- Make some noise. Forget the radio and your CDs and customize your own soundtrack for working out.
- Be well read. Exercise your mind as well as your body with an audiobook.
- Sound off. Try it without the iPod for once, and enjoy the sounds of nature and the neighborhood.

## Home Life

You may hear the "why should we all have to suffer?" defense as you encourage your family to join you on your new and healthier lifestyle. Step back and assess what might be causing that reaction. Fear of giving up the familiar is one possibility. You might also be asking them to do too much too fast, particularly if you were stuck in a pizza, Chinese take-out, and McDonald's routine.

### Start Out Slowly

Try limiting restaurant food to once a week and encouraging healthier menu choices. Instead of mandating "no junk food" off the bat, allow one selection of their choosing to be kept in a cabinet you don't frequent. Above all, work to provide lots of healthy, fresh, and good-tasting alternatives so the change is perceived as a positive one.

If your family members have a favorite food that's a no-no for you, only keep it on hand if you're sure it won't be calling you from the cupboard. Remember, you are not an ogre for requesting that potato chips, moon pies, and Lucky Charms be kept out of the pantry. No matter what degree of pouting and resistance you face from your spouse or children, stand firm. Bypassing these treats won't harm their health; having them could very well hurt yours.

### Make Your Needs Known

It's easy to get discouraged and depressed when others don't seem to be meeting your needs or don't even seem to be aware that you have them. Stop those feelings before they start by laying out exactly what you need from the people around you.

If you find you don't have enough time to exercise as you should because of child care responsibilities, tell your spouse it's essential to your health to get some assistance. If your significant other keeps making you all the things you shouldn't be eating, give her some guidance. Go with her on the next grocery shopping expedition, or, better yet, take her with you on your next appointment with the CDE or dietitian. Don't expect your family and friends to be mind readers. Assume they know next to nothing about your new lifestyle needs, and educate them accordingly.

## No-Sugar Life at Work

If you are employed outside the home, you may need to make some adjustments in your daily work routine to accommodate good treatment habits. There's probably no job out there that is perfectly suited for the no-sugar lifestyle, but there are some employment situations that are more difficult than others. In order to manage your new lifestyle successfully, consider the following options:

- Talk to your doctor about adjustments to your treatment. Could a new medication or insulin regimen help?
- Talk to your boss or manager about adjustments to your work schedule or other accommodations. Is a transfer possible or preferred? Could a shift change be in order?
- Explore your options both inside and outside of your company. If you've been contemplating a career change or return to school, maybe now is the time to get moving.

## Eat, Drink, and Be Wary

Birthday parties, family reunions, wedding receptions, holiday office gatherings—any event where food and drink play a starring role is a potential danger zone without the right preparation. If you know the fare will be high in fat or sugar-rich, bring along a healthy dish (your hostess will probably appreciate the contribution). Having a small snack at home before the event can help to blunt your appetite against too many temptations.

Don't forget that dancing is exercise. Check in with yourself: how do you feel? If you've been out on the dance floor for a while make sure you take a break or get a drink/snack if you need one. If food won't be available at all times during the party, bring a snack with you to fuel up. A non-diet soda or juice from the bar can help to treat a low if you're caught without glucose tablets.

If you decide to enjoy beer, wine, or a mixed drink, use caution and make sure you have a friend with you who knows you well and can help you if you need it.

## On a Road Trip

The minivan, the open road, passing cornfields, roadside diners, the hourly "are we there yet?" question, the carsick baby. Ahhh—the pleasures of the family road trip. Taking a trip by car brings its own unique set of challenges to people living a no-sugar lifestyle. Prolonged sitting, road fatigue, truck stop dining, and should-have-turned-left-at-the-last-exit-but-won't-ask-for-directions syndrome are just a few of the road-blocks you may have to overcome.

Stop and stretch often to get your circulation going and cut fatigue. Again, pack snacks just in case you get waylaid or don't count on the next restaurant being quite so far. A cooler is an excellent idea if you'll be traveling long stretches of remote highways. A cell phone is also essential for rural travel in case a breakdown leaves you stranded or you have a medical emergency.

## Travel Tips for the Wise

Vacations and business travel can present some unique control challenges and safety issues. Don't travel completely alone unless you have to. In case of an emergency, a trusted friend, spouse, or companion will be invaluable, particularly if you're in a foreign country. If you're a free spirit and like to fly solo, make sure you always carry your basic medical information (i.e., name, diagnosis, medication, physician contact) on your person.

## Leisure Travelers

How many times have you returned from a vacation to feel more exhausted and burned out than before you left? Try to lose the "hurry up and have fun—we're paying for this!" attitude and take a trip that involves actual rest and relaxation.

If you're traveling for leisure, try to throw strict schedules (except for those involving food and medication) out the window. Don't stress out and put a damper on your fun. Don't over-plan your days, leave room for flexibility, and enjoy just being in a new environment or culture.

## Business Travelers

Travel for business may throw some unexpected restrictions into your routine. A meeting with a client or an all-day workshop, and suddenly you find yourself behind schedule and going low. You can't work effectively if you don't take care of yourself, so excuse yourself if things run longer than expected. In fact, the best approach is probably to mention a departure time as soon as your meeting begins, and stick to it. If you feel uncomfortable mentioning that you need a time-out to eat or take medication due to your diabetes, then tell your client or colleague you have a dinner or lunch meeting to make (which is entirely true). You can also continue your business over a meal if you feel comfortable doing so.

index